Royce Hanson received his Ph.D. from The American University where he is Associate Professor of Government and Public Administration. Secretary-Treasurer of the National Committee for Fair Representation, and President of the Maryland Committee for Fair Representation, he is also the author of *Fair Representation Comes to Maryland,* and has contributed several articles on the problem of reapportionment to journals and law reviews.

THE POLITICAL THICKET

REAPPORTIONMENT AND
CONSTITUTIONAL DEMOCRACY

Royce Hanson

PRENTICE-HALL, INC.

Englewood Cliffs, New Jersey

To Chester Garfield Hanson and Ila Mae Hanson,
who reared me in the democratic faith,
this book is affectionately dedicated.

P 68555, C 69556

Current printing (last number):
10 9 8 7 6 5 4 3 2 1

FOREWORD

An important element in the success of the American democratic system has been its remarkable facility to meet changing social, economic, and political needs within the basic constitutional framework provided by our Founding Fathers. In the 1930's, for example, we demonstrated our capacity to meet the needs of a new industrial order. Today our educational system is changing to provide higher quality education in greater quantity in response to the demands of science, technology, and the knowledge explosion. The American people have developed an informed and compassionate world outlook in a single generation.

The process of apportioning state legislative bodies is now changing to reflect new patterns of population growth and distribution which have occurred in the past generation.

What has caused these dramatic changes in our population? The technological and transportation revolutions, especially as they have affected rural America, made it possible for people to choose more freely where they would prefer to live and work. Since not all farmers' sons were needed on the land, many chose other vocations elsewhere. Financial and commercial decisions followed these personal choices as business expanded in the growing centers of population. More people traveled to these areas to work in the new industries, to shop in the stores, and to take advantage of the services. Thus, the population shifted—metropolitan areas and suburbs grew; rural areas declined in population. And the shift continues today.

In many states the representation of these growing metropolitan areas in state legislatures has not reflected the population changes. So it is not surprising that citizens streaming into the metropolitan areas became alarmed over their growing inability to function as equal participants in the democratic process. Urbanites and suburbanites could not acquiesce to a situation where they possessed only a half, a tenth, or even a hundredth of the political power held by residents of non-metropolitan areas.

The Supreme Court, speaking in the historic case of *Baker* v.

Carr and subsequent decisions, has responded to this need for more equal representation and has ordered the reapportionment of many state legislatures. Some persons have suggested that these decisions triggered a great political revolution in America. But if it is a revolution, I see it as that special brand of American revolution which seeks to redress wrongs and to correct injustices within the framework of law and through the legal processes of democracy. It is part of the never-ending process of growth and change which has characterized our political and governmental systems from their inception.

Although some people fear that reapportionment of legislatures will result in cities' dominating rural areas, I believe these fears are unfounded. Those familiar with metropolitan politics understand that a wide spectrum of interests exists among urban residents—just as such varied interests exist among people everywhere. Individuals throughout the state will continue to unite in terms of a variety of economic, political, and other interests—seldom will the place of residence, *per se,* provide such a basis.

But the realignment of political forces within a state is likely to produce some resistance and opposition—for no one yields political power voluntarily. For this reason, orderly government has required that institutionalized procedures effect realignment of political power. We provide regular elections for the President and the Congress. Reapportionment among the states in the U. S. House of Representatives is automatically determined by Bureau of the Census calculations.

We are now struggling with the more complex task of devising such procedures for our states. And this task merits priority attention. Orderly and controlled processes of change prevent inequities from accumulating over the years and make change, when it does come, less drastic. The initial jolt of reapportionment in the states would have been much less if there had existed an institutionalized procedure for keeping legislative representation in a more equitable balance with the shifting population.

There still remain unresolved problems concerning the future of reapportionment and equitable representation. When all legislative districts are approximately of equal size, we may discover that many citizens still do not possess the chance to participate in the democratic process on an equal footing with others in their state. Districts may be gerrymandered in a partisan sense so that the minority party has a far smaller proportion of legislators than it has voters in a state. Legislative districts with two or more members may be created. Will this help to give representation to the minority, or will it multiply the influence of a majority voter? These are just a few of the prickly questions that comprise the political thicket of reapportionment.

Some would prefer to avoid these thorns. I believe we have to move forward. Political inequality caused or supported by law cannot be permitted to endure. But we do recognize, of course, that certain other more natural "inequalities" will always endure— members of a legislative body will continue to differ in influence and effectiveness because of their experience, their intellect, their personality, and their character. Farmers, workers, businessmen, professionals, and civic minded people will continue to increase their political authority by joining together in various ways to advance their particular interests. The political party that does the best job in attracting the support of the people—in meeting the needs of society—will continue to grow and prosper at the expense of its opposition.

In short, individuals have many ways of getting their views reflected in the public policy of this country. They do not need the artificial assistance of an unfair reapportionment law to freeze the power relationships of a bygone day.

I am confident that the so-called reapportionment "revolution" will be accomplished within the framework of the American political system—that such traditional virtues as accommodation, pragmatism, flexibility, public understanding, and effective leadership will carry the day.

Then we will recognize clearly the fruits of this victory: a more healthy and responsive political system, better able to serve the needs of the American people in these challenging times.

Professor Hanson's book is a helpful guidepost in this effort.

HUBERT H. HUMPHREY

November, 1965, Washington, D. C.

PREFACE

The battle for fair representation in state legislatures will be the subject of many books. Each state deserves at least one study. Law reviews are already crowded with commentary since the subject is irresistible both for political scientists and for lawyers. I have tried here to write, not *on* reapportionment, but *about* it, because I felt what was needed was less an explanation of the subject itself than an explanation of the way in which American constitutional democracy operates in meeting an issue like reapportionment. My concern, therefore, is not with the technical aspects of apportionment standards or the law cases, but with the significance of the subject as it demonstrates the operation of the political system.

To a considerable extent I have drawn on my personal experience in writing; my methodology has been principally that of the participant observer. My point of view is openly sympathetic to the egalitarian-majoritarian approach to legislative representation, but while trying to make my bias clear, I have also endeavored to separate personal feelings from an analysis of the politics of the problem and of the system. I have concentrated on insight and analysis rather than on description for its own sake.

Since this book was born of experience as well as research, a note on that experience is in order. I have since 1959 been a principal in the Maryland reapportionment movement. From that vantage point I have participated in every aspect of the problem and have been associated with people working on the same problem in other states. Also, I worked on law suits in two states (in one as witness for the plaintiffs), and have helped direct the effort defeating amendment of the United States Constitution to limit the scope of the Supreme Court's reapportionment decisions. Teaching courses in politics at the same time has forced me to try to put my observations into a theoretical perspective.

So this book is not a memoir. It is simply an attempt to show the mutual significance of values, constitutional law, and political practice to our governmental system. It was written because the three elements have rarely been treated jointly; two normally stay in the background while the third is illuminated. My thesis is simple, yet often overlooked in political analysis: An understanding of the American system depends on an appreciation of the way in which these three elements interact in the

ix

decision-making process. The reapportionment problem is just one convenient vehicle for explaining the relationship and illustrating the system.

It is not possible to thank all the people who have aided me in writing this book. My colleagues in the Maryland Committee for Fair Representation gave me the opportunity to play a role in the constitutional drama. Phillip Thorson has been a constant and sagacious counselor. And the years of work with Alfred E. Scanlan, the Committee's general counsel, have been most rewarding. Through our association I was privileged to see a keen legal strategist at work and to share in the development of one of the major cases from its inception in Phil Thorson's living room to its conclusion in the Supreme Court of the United States. In our own suit, and in the Delaware case, I was allowed an inside view of the legal process —as a plaintiff, as a researcher, as an advisor to the attorneys, and finally as a witness—an experience from which I gained new insights into the working of the governmental system. For this I thank Vincent Theisen. I am also in the debt of Governor J. Millard Tawes, who allowed me to participate in much of the decision-making process in Maryland.

For my schooling in legislative lore, I thank the Maryland General Assembly and the Oklahoma legislature, both of which I have been able to observe close at hand, and many of whose members have shared their thoughts and frustrations with me. And particularly am I grateful to Senator Paul Douglas and Senator Joseph D. Tydings, along with Marvin Caplan of the Industrial Union Department, AFL-CIO, for the opportunity given me to participate in the struggle to defeat the Dirksen Amendment.

Jerry Tucker, David Berman, and Marilyn Wenell, as graduate assistants, at various times during the inception and writing of this book gave invaluable assistance in research and criticism.

I give thanks to Mary, who has typed and criticized not only drafts of this manuscript, but of countless other essays, speeches, articles, letters, pamphlets, memoranda, and unenacted bills on reapportionment. Finally, I wish to thank my colleagues at The American University, Daniel Berman, Louis Loeb, and Robert E. Goostree for many helpful suggestions, and Mrs. Barbara Ondrasik, who typed much of the manuscript.

TABLE OF CONTENTS

INTRODUCTION

All animals are equal, but some are more equal than others.

George Orwell
Animal Farm

When you got the votes, you can do anything you want.

State Senator Harvey T. Phoebus, Maryland

Jesse Maury was angry. "Something ought to be done. I'll sue!" Jesse had just realized he had been shortchanged by his own state. And for no reason. He was as good as most Marylanders—maybe better than most. He was a college graduate, a professional engineer, a business executive, a taxpayer, and was active in civic and party affairs. He lived in the Washington suburbs with people of comparable backgrounds and attainments. And they were shortchanged the same as he. How?

They all could vote. But what was the effect of that vote? With eleven per cent of the state's voters in 1960, Maury's county had less than four per cent of the voting strength in the state legislature. If he had chosen to live in a nearby rural county instead of the suburbs—doing the same work, paying the same taxes—Maury would have had his individual influence as a voter increased by over twenty-two times. Somehow this made no sense.

Then there were the practical consequences. The legislature set the tax rate and the tax equalization formulas. Why should the people in the small counties have more power to set the tax rate through their representatives than he had, and to decide how the taxes should be spent? Why should the counties with over half the registered automobiles receive only an eighth of the state highway revenues for secondary roads when state commissions repeatedly urged a change in the 1923 formula on which the revenue alloca-

1

tions were based? How could the state legislature restrict the unemployment compensation laws when Senators representing over eighty percent of the people voted to liberalize them? Why couldn't there be a state law against racial discrimination in public accomodations? Why did the majority of the citizens of Maryland have to sit and take it silently when the Eastern Shore caucus put into practice the words of their chorus:

> We don't give a damn for the whole State of Maryland,
> We're from the Eastern Shore.

Halfway across the continent a young lawyer, C. H. Spearman, Jr., sitting in the gallery of the Oklahoma House of Representatives and watching a vote on sales tax exemptions for feed, seed and fertilizer, thought much the same as Maury. "C'mon you short grass boys, let's show 'em where the votes are," whooped a red-faced representative from the panhandle.

In Nashville, Tennessee, Mayor Ben West mused that one of Tennessee's rural counties contained 3611 cows, 4739 pigs and horses, 3948 people, and one representative. Davidson County had 381,412 inhabitants and seven representatives, which meant that each representative spoke for 54,487 people, but not, of course, for many cows, horses, and pigs.[1]

And in Lansing, Michigan, Governor G. Mennen Williams found that in spite of his impressive victories in six consecutive elections, and in spite of the support of legislators representing a majority of the state's voters, he could not obtain enactment of badly needed tax revisions. As a result the state was unable to meet its payroll. Why was Michigan's legislature, like New York's, "constitutionally Republican"? [2]

In most other states the questions which worried Maury, Spearman, Mayor West, and Governor Williams were repeatedly asked. Why? The "Next Election," reported *Harper's*, "is Already Rigged." [3]

The legislatures of most states distributed, or *apportioned* representatives in such a fashion that a minority of the population elected a majority of seats in one or both houses. That Maury and

---

[1] "Unrepresentatives," *The New Republic* (Jan. 29, 1963), p. 3.
[2] Gus Tyler and David J. Wells, "New York: Constitutionally Republican" in Malcolm E. Jewell, ed. *The Politics of Reapportionment* (New York: Atherton Press, 1962), pp. 221-248.
[3] Richard Lee Strout, "The Next Election is Already Rigged," *Harper's* (November 1959), p. 35.

others thought it unfair was a natural reaction for citizens reared on tales of the Boston Tea Party and the Revolution's cry of "No Taxation without Representation," the Declaration of Independence, and the Gettysburg Address. The perversion of the ideal of political equality by the harsh reality of legislative malapportionment seemed downright un-American.

In the United States today there is a confluence of political theory, constitutional law, and practical politics in the process of making democratic politics constitutional and in making constitutional law democratic. American legislatures have been criticized and their procedures altered by the efforts of people like Jesse Maury, Mayor West and other citizens, politicians, and lawyers. An examination of the growth and development of our state legislatures will help us understand how they became the way they did in the middle of the 20th century and will highlight the political and constitutional processes which changed them.

THE RISE AND FALL
OF REPRESENTATIVE GOVERNMENT

Time makes ancient good uncouth.

James Russell Lowell

There is a pleasant fiction that political theory and political practice proceed in mutual ignorance of each other. It may be that the relationship of theory and practice is sometimes imperceptible, but it is rarely nonexistent. Philosophy and ideology condition what is done in politics, how it is done, and how it is explained. Theory provides the basis for judging the propriety of public actions and evaluating their impact on other things of value, such as "freedom," "security," or "welfare."

The practical politician employs theory as a tool for the justification of his actions or as a lever to rally public support for his cause. Theory is also shaped by events. What seems "good" in practice tends to lead toward the abandonment of ideas which suggested that it was "bad." Similarly, concepts of what is *constitutional*—that is, basic to the way government is formed and works—is conditioned by political ideas and by practical political experience. As ideas and experience change, so do constitutions, frequently without so much as the dropping of a comma. If constitutions will not change, amendment or even revolution may be needed.

A constitution also influences theory and politics. It may generate theory from the need to explain it. It may shape politics by what it permits and what it forbids.

The close relationship among theory, law, and politics can be seen in many areas of national life, but in few is it focused as dramatically as in the issue of state legislative apportionment. There the theory and practice of representative government grew together for many years and then separated. From this division new ideas and new political needs arose. What is striking in the history of representation is the paradox of an ever-expanding concept of

4

political equality in America, and, following the split of theory and practice at the turn of the 20th century, the steady erosion of equal representation in state legislatures.

This paradox complicates analysis but illustrates the problem of interpreting the constitutionality of representation schemes. From the mixture of theory, state constitutions, and historical experience, two members of the Supreme Court of the United States derived two thoroughly antagonistic constitutional, theoretical and practical "traditions" of representation in America.

In *Gray* v. *Sanders*, Mr. Justice William O. Douglas wrote for the majority of the Court that

> The conception of political equality from the Declaration of Independence, to Lincoln's Gettysburg Address, to the Fifteenth, Seventeenth, and Nineteenth Amendments can mean only one thing—one person, one vote.[1]

But reviewing the same history, Mr. Justice Felix Frankfurter vigorously dissented in the Tennessee apportionment case, *Baker* v. *Carr*:

> The notion that representation proportioned to the geographic spread of population is . . . "The basic principle of representative government" is, to put it bluntly, not true. However desirable and however desired among the great political thinkers and framers of our government, it has never been generally practiced, today or in the past. It was not the English system, it was not the colonial system, it was not the system chosen for the national government by the Constitution, it was not the system exclusively or even predominantly practiced by the states at the time of the adoption of the Fourteenth Amendment, and it is not predominantly practiced by the states today.[2]

REPRESENTATION
IN COLONIAL AND REVOLUTIONARY AMERICA

Colonial America advanced the idea of representative government more swiftly than did English government. In part this may have resulted from experience with colonial church government and from the embellishment of the institution of directors in the trading companies.

[1] *Gray* v. *Sanders*, 372 U.S. 368, 381 (1963).
[2] *Baker* v. *Carr*, 369 U.S. 186, 301 (1962).

The requirements of exercising political power in the colonies proved to be different from those existing in England. The basis of support for a nobility and a system of social ranking was difficult to find or to defend in a raw new land with endless frontiers. As a practical matter the colonists demanded some participation in their government as a price for submission to royal authority. This insistence, backed by the political doctrines of John Locke and the English revolutionaries of the seventeenth century and combined with selected egalitarian implications of Protestant theology, drove the colonial governments toward expansion of representative institutions—town governments, legislative assemblies, and the freehold suffrage. As early as 1635, town representation in the General Court of Massachusetts bore a crude relationship to population.

Two traditions of representation find their origins in colonial America. Representation based on population began to be practiced, but there was also a strong tendency to represent towns and jurisdictions. The practical effect of the latter was not great, since in most colonies variations in the size of communities were not great. But even in the colonial period, the westward expansion of the colonies caused a few serious apportionment problems as the tidewater towns resisted efforts of the frontier settlements for a larger share of political power in the colonial assemblies.[3]

Another important practice with its origins in colonial representative institutions was *bicameralism.* Growing in part out of antipathy between the colonial governors and the representative bodies elected from the voters in the colonies, most colonial legislative assemblies eventually were divided into an elected assembly and a governor's council. While the Commons-Lords analogy is an attractive *post hoc* explanation, it seems more likely that jealousies over power, such as that which caused the Virginia Burgesses to refuse to sit with the Council in a common chamber, offer a more realistic explanation of the origins of bicameralism.[4] The existence of a second chamber in most of the colonies did, however, have considerable effect upon political thought about representative institu-

---

[3] See Allan Nevins, *The American States During and After the Revolution, 1775-1789* (New York: The Macmillan Company, 1927), chap. 1; Alfred De Grazia, *Public and Republic* (New York: Alfred A. Knopf, Inc., 1951), pp. 60-61; "Minutes of the Provincial Council of Pennsylvania," IX, 138ff., Henry Steele Commager, ed., *Documents of American History,* 5th ed. (New York: Appleton-Century-Crofts, Inc., 1949), p. 50.

[4] See Robert Luce, *Legislative Assemblies* (Boston: Houghton Mifflin Company, 1924), pp. 4-21.

tions once independence from Britain was asserted. Few framers of the new governments doubted the superiority of two legislative chambers over one. Of the major statesmen of the era, only Benjamin Franklin was a vigorous exponent of unicameralism.

The practice of popular government and representation in the colonies fused conveniently with the necessities of revolutionary politics and polemics. The British assertion that the colonies were virtually represented in Parliament could hardly have excited less colonial sympathy. Daniel Dulany, a revolutionary pamphleteer, clearly stated the attitude of many colonists against the idea that it was unimportant that America had no direct representatives at Westminster since they were adequately represented simply by virtue of being English. Dulany denounced the theory of virtual representation as "fantastical and frivolous nonsense . . . the most contemptible idea that ever entered into the head of a man; it does not deserve serious refutation." [5]

The theory of direct representation became a principal tool of the revolutionary pamphleteers in their criticism of British rule. Only a legislature directly chosen by the people could levy taxes, they argued. This, they held, was simply an extension to America of the historic rights of British subjects. [6]

In the 1760's John Adams argued that the legislature should represent the people and be directly controlled by them:

It [the representative body] should be in miniature an exact portrait of the people at large. It should think, feel, reason, and act like them. That it may be the interest of this assembly to do strict justice at all times, it should be an equal representation, or, in other words, equal interests among the people should have equal interests in it. [7]

Adams spoke the dominant view of his day. The " 'right of representation' was the basic right of political man, the right 'on which all other rights essentially depend.' " [8]

Even Alexander Hamilton adhered to the doctrines of direct representation in the legislature both before the revolution and at

[5] See Merrill Jensen, "Commentary," in Randolph Adams, *Political Ideas of the American Revolution,* 3rd ed. (New York: Barnes & Noble, Inc., 1958), pp. 14-15.

[6] Jensen, in *Political Ideas, op. cit.,* pp. 10-15.

[7] Clinton Rossiter, *Seed-Time of the Republic* (New York: Harcourt, Brace & World, Inc., 1953), p. 390.

[8] *New Hampshire Gazette,* March 18, 1774, as quoted in Rossiter, *Seed-Time of the Republic, op. cit.,* p. 389.

the federal constitutional convention. There he stood in the early days of the convention with James Madison and James Wilson, urging that "the rights of suffrage in the National Legislature ought to be proportioned to the number of free inhabitants." [9]

The doctrine of equal representation had no spokesman more influential than Thomas Jefferson. In his *Notes on Virginia* and in his letters on government he consistently pursued the idea of equality of representation as a basic ingredient of republican government.

While it is true that he deprecated the talents of city dwellers for self-government, he gave John Locke's doctrine of consent of the governed its most eloquent expression in the Declaration of Independence. He lamented Virginia's malapportionment, and in a letter to William King of Maine commenting on the new constitution of that state he wrote:

> Equal representation is so fundamental a principle in a true republic that no prejudices can justify its violation, because the prejudices themselves cannot be justified. [10]

The revolutionary fervor for equal representation is reflected in the first state constitutions. While population was not always the explicit basis for legislative representation, it was the most pervasive factor applied by the states. Even where it was not used, the resulting representative systems were not grossly out of proportion with the dispersion of the population. [11]

Delaware, New Jersey, and Maryland all based representation on counties, but the first census, taken in 1790, showed a rather small difference in the populations of the counties. [12]

It would not be fair to suggest that the newly independent states invariably followed clear principles in apportioning their legislatures. In New Jersey, for example, equal representation of counties in the senate was established as a quick means of finishing work on the 1776 constitution so delegates could flee the capital before British troops marched on them from their landing at Sandy Hook. The significant element is the extent to which population was

[9] Richard B. Morris, *Alexander Hamilton and the Founding of the Nation* (New York: The Dial Press, Inc., 1957), p. 1145.
[10] *Jefferson Papers,* Library of Congress, vol. 216 (November 19, 1819), 38616.
[11] Advisory Commission on Intergovernmental Relations, *Apportionment of State Legislatures* (Washington, D.C.: U.S. Government Printing Office, 1962), p. 7.
[12] Advisory Commission, *Apportionment, Ibid.,* p. 7.

used and the extent to which its use was advocated as the "proper" basis for representation. The power of the idea of popular representation was also reflected in the Northwest Ordinance, enacted in 1787, the same year the Constitution was submitted to the states for ratification. Adopted unanimously by Congress, it provided for a direct relationship between population and representation in the territorial legislatures and in the legislatures of the states which might be carved out of the great territory.

The federal constitutional convention is viewed by some writers as a conservative reaction to the revolutionary era. In most ways this is a fair appraisal, but *not* in the case of state legislative representation. While the Great Compromise creating the U.S. Senate and giving equal representation to the states has often been regarded as a response to the "balance of forces" theory of representation, the evidence of the convention itself suggests another explanation. The Great Compromise represented, as Madison pointed out in No. 62 of the *Federalist,* not a theory, but a spirit of compromise necessary to the establishment of the union. The theory came later to justify the compromise.

There is impressive evidence from the records of the federal convention and the state ratifying conventions that both the advocates of direct popular representation for the two houses of the new Congress and those who favored equal representation of states in the Senate were in agreement that in unitary governments such as existed within the separate states, representation in both houses should be based upon population.[13]

THE EPIDEMIC OF POLITICAL EQUALITY: FROM THE CONSTITUTION TO THE CIVIL WAR

The example of the federal constitution had little, if any, effect on either the theory or practice of state legislative representation for a hundred years after its adoption.[14] The states created from the Northwest Territory used a population basis for representation in each house of their respective legislatures. Other newly admitted

[13] This point of view is extensively set forth in *Appendix B to the Brief for the United States as Amicus Curiae Maryland Committee for Fair Representation* v. *Tawes,* No. 29, October 1963, Supreme Court of the United States; See especially pp. 89ff.

[14] See Luce, *Legislative Assemblies, op. cit.,* pp. 47-59.

states also reflected the trend toward political equality which was accelerated by the ideals of Jeffersonian democracy and the Jacksonian impulses toward expanded suffrage and direct democracy. It is hardly fair to describe as "theory" the approach to representation of the Jacksonians. In part it was ideology, but more than anything else, democracy became a folk movement.

The federal Constitution was not a document which expressed great confidence in unfettered democracy. But however the constitutional philosophy of Hamilton and John Marshall prospered in the development of national government, their views were steadily overridden in the state governments. Not only the new states entering the union but also the revised constitutions in the original states reflected the growth of democratic sentiment. In Virginia John Marshall was overridden at the 1820 convention by the advocates of popular sovereignty and representation of population. In New York Chancellor Kent protested in vain the extension of suffrage at the 1821 convention, and in Massachusetts Daniel Webster lost his fight to retain the property qualification for voting for state senators. Mixed government was not regarded as suitable for state democracy, and bicameralism was not regarded as requiring different bases of representation for the separate houses.[15]

Thomas Lincoln, in an historic debate on representation in the senate at the Massachusetts convention in 1820, expressed the prevailing attitude of the democrats:

> Representation is founded on the interests of the people. It is because they have rights that they have assumed the power of self-government . . . It is only necessary that all who are taxed should be represented, and not that they should be represented in proportion to their tax.[16]

Even in conservative states such as Maryland, the democrats made progress. In 1837 the electoral college system of electing senators was changed to provide for direct election and a weighted population formula was adopted for election of members of the House of Delegates. Throughout the nation agitation for reform in suffrage and representation was extensive. Major battles between the Jacksonian and the Whig views erupted in Louisiana and in other states. In general the trend toward direct and equal representation was a

[15] See Arthur N. Holcombe, *State Government in the United States,* 3rd ed. (New York: The Macmillan Company, 1934), p. 284.
[16] Alpheus Mason, *Free Government in the Making,* 2d ed. (New York: Oxford University Press, 1956), p. 389.

part of the egalitarian impetus of Jacksonian democracy, which produced elected judges, prosecutors, and even surveyors and coroners.

Again, in spite of the now universal use of bicameralism in the states' governments, there seemed to be no emulation of the federal basis of representation as a model. Writing in the 1830's, Alexis de Tocqueville observed of the state legislatures:

> The members of the two houses are nearly everywhere subject to the same conditions of eligibility. They are chosen in the same manner, and by the same citizens. . . .
> By this separation of the legislative body into two branches, the Americans plainly did not desire to make one house hereditary and the other elective, one aristocratic and the other democratic. It was not their object to create in the one a bulwark to power, while the other represented the interests and passions of the people. The only advantages that result from the present constitution of the two houses in the United States are the division of the legislative power, and the consequent check upon political movements, together with the creation of a tribunal of appeal for the revision of the laws.[17]

Twenty states joined the union between the ratification of the Constitution and the Civil War. Only two, Vermont and Florida, provided a basis other than population for representation in either house of their legislatures.[18]

THE AGE
OF DIRECT REPRESENTATION

The immediate impact of the Civil War on representation was to buttress both the doctrine and practice of direct representation. The Civil War amendments to the federal constitution expanded suffrage by ostensibly abolishing racial qualifications. While there is no direct evidence that the reconstruction amendments were intended to improve the representativeness of state legislatures beyond extending the vote to Negroes, their effect was to do so.

The reconstruction constitutions, abandoning both race and property as bases of representation, were uniformly more democratic

---

[17] Alexis de Tocqueville, *Democracy in America* (New York: Vintage Press, 1955), p. 87.
[18] Advisory Commission, *Apportionment, op. cit.,* pp. 9-10.

than those they replaced. These restrictive provisions were generally replaced by language making the whole population the basis for apportionment.[19]

Throughout the reconstruction and post-reconstruction period, revised constitutions in the older states as well as the constitutions of the newly admitted states increasingly provided for a population basis for representation and for universal manhood suffrage. The 1864 Constitution of Maryland, for instance, provided for a reasonably fair population base for the lower house, and in the 1867 Constitution population was recognized as a factor in senate representation by giving additional senators to Baltimore.

National policy seemed to reflect the spreading confidence in popular democracy. In the creation of territories in the West, Congress uniformly provided in the organic acts for legislatures based on population. Normally the language of the organic acts incorporated or echoed the general statutes on territories:

> The apportionment of representation . . . shall be as nearly equal as practicable among the several districts and counties for such first election of the council and house of representatives, giving to each section of the territory representation in the ratio of its population, except Indians not taxed; and thereafter in such new territory, as well as in all territories now organized, the legislative assemblies, respectively, may re-adjust and apportion the representation to the two houses thereof and among the several counties and districts, in such manner from time to time, as they deem just and proper . . .[20]

The real significance of this provision is that its basic proposition was followed in the original apportionment provisions of the states admitted to the Union after 1868. Only two, New Mexico and Montana, ignored population in one house of their legislatures, and the disparities in these states were not great at the time of their admission. Idaho provided for equal representation of counties in its senate but grouped counties in its initial apportionment. All other states admitted before World War I based both their houses fully or substantially on population.

Some constitutions, like Oklahoma's, contrived restrictions on the number of representatives or senators a county might have. These provisions operated to produce grossly discriminatory apportion-

---

[19] Ellis Merton Coulter, *The South During Reconstruction, 1865-77*, VIII, in *A History of the South* (Baton Rouge, La.: Louisiana State University Press, 1947), p. 135.

[20] Sec. 1849, *Rev. Stat. of 1878*, (Title 23, Ch. I).

ments many years later, but at the time of admission, representation was reasonably related to population.[21]

The period now under consideration was one in which popular democracy was a major, if not the dominant, political movement shaping state institutions. This was the period which saw the birth of the cooperative movement, the Populist Party, the Progressive Party, and the demand for extension of democracy through the initiative, the referendum, and the recall. The indirect election of U.S. Senators came under increasing attack as did the exclusion of women from voting, situations which ultimately led to national constitutional amendments.

There seems, in fact, to have been little dispute during this period whether population should be the basis of representation, just as there was no dispute over the truism that bicameralism works best. Woodrow Wilson, comparing state and federal bicameralism at the turn of the century, found

> There is . . . no such historical reason [as the Connecticut compromise] for having two houses in the states as exists in the case of the federal government. The object of the federal arrangement is the representation of the two elements upon which the national government rests, namely, the popular will and a federal union of states. The state legislatures have two houses simply for purposes of deliberateness in legislation, in order, that is, that legislation may be filtered through the debates of two coordinate bodies, representing slightly differing constituencies, though coming both directly from the people, and may thus escape the taint of precipitation too apt to attach to the conclusions of a single all-powerful popular chamber. The double organization represents no principle, but only an effort at prudence.[22]

So far as representation was concerned, the issue of the time was not the basis of apportionment but rather the adequacy of the single member district system of electing representatives, as compared with proportional representation in the state legislatures. P.R. became a favorite nostrum of reform writers and politicians such as John R. Commons and Horace Greeley.[23]

But the argument over P.R. was not in the main stream of either political thought or action. The real question was that of partici-

[21] Advisory Commission, *Apportionment, op. cit.*, pp. 9-10.
[22] Woodrow Wilson, *The State*, rev. ed. (Boston: D.C. Heath & Company, 1902), pp. 487-88.
[23] For a discussion of the proportional representation movement in America see De Grazia, *Public and Republic, op. cit.*, pp. 184-204.

pation—how to get people involved, informed, and effective. The obsession was to "make democracy work," curing its ills with more democracy. One writer on the history of representation in America has noted that "if the post Civil War period in America can be called the Age of Insurgency, it may also be called the Age of Reaction of Direct Representation." [24]

The same forces which generated democratic sentiment and progressive reforms generated opposition to their endeavors. Basically, the reformers and democrats sought to make use of traditional theories and the existing governmental machinery. They were propelled by the logic of democracy mixed with a growing sense of outrage against the "establishment" of the day. The establishment, on the other hand, was not ready to surrender, and it still controlled the main points of power. Thus, exceptions to the democratic rule began to appear in the constitutions of the 1890's.

Delaware's leaders successfully fought off a population basis for representation. In Ohio, Mark Hanna's Republicans amended the state constitution. The "Hanna Amendment" simply provided that each county would always be entitled to one representative. With 88 counties and 100 representatives, the Hanna forces would be assured of control. In New York and Pennsylvania, the new constitutions established restrictive formulas for apportionment openly designed to preclude urban domination of the legislatures. In other states, restrictions on equal representation, such as minimum guarantees for all counties or maximum limits on the representation of any county, which had been of little consequence when adopted, were beginning to have a noticeable, if not appreciable, effect by the end of the second decade of the 20th century.

REVERSING THE TREND

In 1920 the urban population of the United States exceeded the rural population for the first time. The national trend was reflected in many states. The impact of this fact on the politics of representation can be seen in the increasing refusal of state legislatures to reapportion themselves, even if the state constitution "required" it. Since 1920 few additional states have adopted popular "reforms" such as the initiative, referendum, or recall. And only a

[24] *Ibid.*, p. 160.

few states—Missouri, New Jersey, Tennessee, and Michigan—have held constitutional conventions since 1912. In both New Jersey and Tennessee, the call of the convention by the legislatures precluded full consideration of the apportionment problem. This exclusion of representation from consideration reflected the fear of incumbent legislators that a convention might reapportion.

The primary reasons for the increase of disparities in representation in the state legislatures fell into three basic categories which can be illustrated from state experience:

1. *Deliberate failure to implement constitutional provisions.* States such as Alabama, Tennessee, and Oklahoma did not reapportion even though their constitutions specifically required it and established formulas for its accomplishment. Frequently, the decennial reapportionment act, if passed at all by the legislature, simply re-enacted the old distribution of seats. An analysis of the apportionment problem written in 1938 noted that "inequalities in senate districts in twenty-six states [were] due primarily to legislative inaction, in contrast to only fifteen states where the constitutional provisions are primarily responsible for the inequalities." [25]

2. *Outgrowing the constitution and refusing to change it.* In a number of states the population simply outgrew the state constitutions. Apportionments that were once fair were now grotesque as legislatures refused to initiate constitutional amendments. Iowa, Kansas, Florida, Georgia, Maryland, Delaware, Vermont, and Rhode Island were among the states where disparities increased with each decade. These states all rigorously adhered to their state constitutions, but implementation of the formulas themselves, as in New York or Pennsylvania, constituted a discriminatory act as a result of both population growth and shifts in population concentration.

3. *Changing the constitution to produce malapportionment.* Many states, as indicated above, had constitutional provisions requiring regular and equitable reapportionment. Had the provisions stood, change would have followed, so the incumbent legislatures occasionally sought to amend the constitutions to maintain the status quo in the distribution of power. Such amendments, sold as "balanced representation" or as "the best compromise to be obtained," or as schemes to "protect minority rights," were adopted in Michigan, California, and Illinois. In each case, "non-population"

[25] David O. Walter, "Reapportionment and Urban Representation," *The Annals of the American Academy of Political and Social Science*, 195 (January 1938), 13.

factors were introduced into the apportionment plan for at least one house. In Michigan, this consisted of freezing the 1920 population-based apportionment into the constitution.

After 1920 only a few states made changes to make representation more equitable. Oregon was a notable exception, along with Wisconsin. Virginia acted to implement its fair constitutional language until 1950, when full implementation would possibly have damaged the existing distribution of power by giving heavier gains to the Norfolk and the Arlington-Alexandria areas. While still better apportioned than most states, regression in representativeness began in Virginia also. The general tendency of the time was toward increasing disparities in representation.

By 1960 a second transformation in the national population was evident. Now the suburban population began to equal, and in many states to exceed, that of the central cities. Moreover, central city population was declining and that of the suburbs was increasing at a rapid rate. As living in metropolis became the "American way of life," areas which had joined the rural counties in the reapportionment battles of the 1930's and 1940's to keep down the power of the cities were now the principal victims of their earlier handiwork.

Conditions both in legislatures and in congressional districts had reached a state of extreme disparity in many states. A study completed in 1962 found that between 1937 and 1955, thirty-seven legislatures had become less representative of the population in their states.[26]

Dissatisfaction grew with the disparities. Reapportionment became a mounting concern of those interested in effective state government. The U.S. Commission on Intergovernmental Relations in its 1955 report to President Dwight D. Eisenhower considered malapportionment a major cause of the decline of state government in the federal system. "The Commission has come to the conclusion," the President was told, "that the more the role of the States in our system is emphasized, the more important it is that the State legislatures be reasonably representative of all the people."[27]

The problem was also reflected in the attention given it by the

[26] Paul T. David and Ralph Eisenberg, *The Devaluation of the Urban and Suburban Vote* (Charlottesville, Va.: University of Virginia Press, 1961), p. 6.
[27] Commission on Intergovernmental Relations, *A Report to the President for Transmittal to Congress* (Washington, D.C.: U.S. Government Printing Office, 1955), p. 40.

popular press and by public officials. In 1958 Senator John F. Kennedy called malapportionment the "Shame of the States," [28] and in 1960 Senator Joseph S. Clark (Dem., Pa.) proposed an amendment to the U.S. Constitution to require periodic and equitable reapportionment of state legislatures.[29] Such organizations as the U.S. Conference of Mayors and the National Municipal League also became actively interested in finding a solution to the problem.

The problem was not new. Its dimensions were. The idea of political equality had not noticeably relaxed its hold on the American imagination, but the practice of political equality seemed destined to vanish in the legislatures, those bodies thought by the framers of the constitutions to be "closest to the people."

"[It] often comes to pass," wrote the philosopher John Locke in 1689,

> . . . that in tract of time . . . representation becomes very unequal
> and disproportionate to the reasons it was first established upon . . .
> To what gross absurdities the following of custom may lead . . . when
> we see the bare name of a town of which there remains not so much
> as a ruins, where scarce so much as a sheepcote or more inhabitants
> than a shepherd is to be found, sends so many representatives to the
> grand assembly of lawmakers as a whole county numerous in people
> and powerful in riches. This strangers stand amazed at, and everyone
> must confess needs a remedy; though most find it hard to find one,
> because . . . no inferior power can alter [the legislature] . . . And,
> therefore, . . . this inconvenience is thought incapable of a remedy.[30]

[28] *New York Times Magazine,* May 18, 1958, p. 38.
[29] S.J. Res. 215, 86th Congress, 2d Session (1960).
[30] John Locke, *The Second Treatise of Civil Government,* par. 157.

IMPASSE OF DEMOCRACY

When my people get tired of me they
can vote me out of office, but I'll be
damned if I'll vote myself out.

Delegate Earl Bennett
Maryland House of Delegates, 1962

The theory and practice of representative government in the American states did not square. The rising disparities in representation were increasingly met by intransigence against change. The impasse against which John Locke warned in 1690 had been reached in 20th century America. The legislatures refused by their action or inaction to implement the constitutional systems which gave them existence and the principles of democracy which gave them meaning. Against this cold fact of politics, even sophisticated observers like H. L. Mencken expressed amazement, disbelief, and disgust.

In 1928, in a wide-ranging article on the struggle of urban against rural interests, he wrote

> The yokels hang on because old apportionments give them unfair advantages. The vote of a malarious peasant on the lower Eastern Shore counts as much as the votes of twelve Baltimoreans. But that can't last. It is not only unjust and undemocratic; it is absurd.[1]

Although the situation was easily stereotyped to fit the frustrations of urbanists like Mencken, city politicians, and government reformers, the reasons for its existence are not as simple as they seemed. Many factors were involved: the struggle between city and rural based interests and politicians, outright partisanship, the character of state legislatures themselves, and the strange political psychology of the reapportionment issue. All these factors conspired

[1] Malcolm Moos, ed., *H. L. Mencken on Politics: A Carnival of Buncombe* (New York: Vintage Books, 1960), p. 164.

18

with the demonstrably difficult problem of devising a specific plan which was "fair" to all concerned, and made futile the mounting cries for reform and the sporadic forays against malapportionment.

CITY AGAINST COUNTRY:
MYTH AND REALITY

The reason most frequently advanced for the persistence of malapportionment can be inferred from Mencken's ephithet, "Barnyard Government"—a blind grasping for political power by rural legislators to prevent an increase of urban influence in state politics. Certainly hostility to cities was a major factor in apportionment politics. While the constitutional conventions of the early 19th century had been torn by rival claims to representation by the rich and the poor, those of the late 19th and early 20th century were concerned with the preservation of power in the hands of the representatives of the tillers of the soil and the small townsmen. To an inherent agrarian bias were added blatant prejudices against racial, national, and religious minorities populating the cities.

A delegate to the New York constitutional convention of 1864 argued for containment of New York City's representation:

> I say without fear of contradiction . . . that the average citizen in the rural district is superior in intelligence, superior in morality, superior in self-government, to the average citizen in the great cities.
>
> . . . I tell you, gentlemen, you who represent the great city, that when that time comes, when your streets are filled with those who defy the law, when socialists, when those who believe in no government, are parading your streets and destroying your property and killing your citizens, then you will cry for help. And to whom? You will then turn your eyes to the green fields of Oneida and Herkimer and Jefferson and St. Lawrence. You will call to us, we who have no Emma Goldbergs and no Herr Mosts . . .[2]

At the 1874 Pennsylvania convention, restrictions on Philadelphia's representation which had been written into the 1838 Constitution under the leadership of Thaddeus Stevens were kept in altered form. The city was never to receive more than one-sixth of

[2] *Revised Record of the New York State Constitutional Convention* (1894), pp. 10-11.

the representation in the senate. Even then, Philadelphia contained a fifth of the state's population. Experience, Judge George Woodward remarked, had shown that great cities did not send to the legislature men who represented "the intellect, culture, and enterprise" of the community. Woodward's remarks suggested that he viewed the city as a parasite living off the virtuous rural areas.[3]

These statements are not atypical of those expressed in other constitutional conventions or in state legislatures facing reapportionment problems. By the early years of the 20th century, hostility toward the city and the interests based there had become a standard "reason" for the existence of malapportionment and for its deliberate maintenance. Limits on the number of representatives any area might have became increasingly common as did failure of legislatures to reapportion at all.[4]

Malapportionment was increasingly expressed in terms of urban-rural conflict and measured accordingly. However, the coincidence of urban growth and malapportionment, while quite significant, also tends to obscure much when one attempts to understand reasons for the persistence of unrepresentative government.

First, the conflict was almost as much myth as reality. American political thought contains a heavy bias against the city. The most influential treatise on national development, Frederick Jackson Turner's *The Frontier in American History*, is not a history of urban growth, which might be considered the dominant change in American society since the Civil War. However much Turner overemphasized the role of the frontier, it still has played more on the American imagination than the building of cities. It was Davy Crockett and Wild Bill Hickock rather than Big Bill Thompson or Boss Tweed who became folk heroes, although their respective derring-do and moral fibre seem roughly comparable.

America's greatness seemed derived from the soil, the forests, the open country, and not from the commercial and mental activity of her cities.[5] Had not Jefferson himself maintained the superiority of an agrarian life? A view no more admirably put is that by the

[3] Rosalind L. Branning, *Pennsylvania, Constitutional Development* (Pittsburgh: University of Pittsburgh Press, 1960), p. 71.
[4] Gordon E. Baker, *State Constitutions: Reapportionment* (New York: National Municipal League, 1960), p. 4.
[5] For a brief but cogent summary of the agrarian mythology of the city, see Anselm L. Strauss, *Images of the American City* (New York: The Free Press of Glencoe, 1961), pp. 167-182.

Great Commoner, William Jennings Bryan, in his Cross of Gold speech in 1896:

> Burn down your cities and leave our farms, and your cities will spring up again as if by magic; but destroy our farms and grass will grow in the streets of every city in the country.[6]

Bryan spoke in the grand tradition of bias against the city. Tocqueville, fifty years earlier, had seen the growth of cities as a danger to democracy because of the volatile elements they contained. He gave the legislator, reluctant to reapportion, an eloquent intellectual framework for his reflection of the instinctive fear of the agrarian for the metropolis.

"To subject the provinces to the metropolis," he argued, "would place the destiny of the empire not only in the hands of a portion of the community, which is unjust, but in the hands of a populace carrying out its own impulses, which is very dangerous." [7]

To give a preponderance of power to the great cities would be "a serious injury to the representative system." The republics of antiquity perished, he asserted, from the domination by their capital cities.[8]

For many an American intellectual, the city was a dirty and evil place. Only from the open air to the west and in the rich soil of the new world might the distinctive, creative, American spirit flourish. James Fenimore Cooper's popular *Leather Stockings Tales* and his *The American Democrat* gave both intellectual and romantic sustenance to the agrarian frontier myth. The city and virtue seemed incompatible.

There was, unfortunately, enough evidence to sustain the view. American cities in the post-bellum period were neither sanitary nor democratic idylls. The problems of the city, glutted with immigrants and freed Negroes, ridden with corruption, smoke and gangsters, provided dramatic reinforcement for stereotypes of urban life and politics. Nothing could have been more tailored to repel the "True American." Lord Bryce's indictment of city government as America's "one conspicuous failure" [9] and Lincoln Steffens' car-

---

[6] "Bryan's Cross of Gold Speech," in Henry Steele Commager, ed., *Documents of American History, op. cit.*, p. 50.
[7] Alexis de Tocqueville, *Democracy in America* (New York: Vintage Press, 1945), I, 299-300.
[8] *Ibid.*, p. 300.
[9] William Bryce, *The American Commonwealth*, 2nd ed. (Commonwealth Publishing Co., 1890), p. 681.

bolic criticism, *The Shame of the Cities*,[10] provided more evidence of the incapacity of the urban population to share fully in the tasks of self-government.

Instinctive fears were augmented by the political fears engendered by the rise of the boss system in city politics. Over-representation of rural areas could be rationalized as a means of keeping the monsters in check. The bosses themselves seemed not to mind too much, often finding ways to work through pliable rural members while enjoying effective control at home.[11] But the important point was that a disciplined machine, driven by an avaricious boss, if given full representation, might run the state its own way—the farmers be damned! Long after the power of the bosses was dispersed among lesser political figures—1/6 Bosses, as the cartoonist Yardley draws Baltimore's lingering district leaders—malapportionment could be justified as a balancing of interests required for good government: a balance of rural against urban, of virtue against unprincipled power, of the minority against the majority.

The fear was not without substance. The myth needed no evidence and heeded none to the contrary. Before the ascendancy of small town bosses and lawyers in rural politics, the patricians and country gentlemen from the sparsely populated areas presented a sharp contrast in the legislature to the barely literate ward heelers and petty grafters all too frequently among the city legislative delegation. In *The American Commonwealth*, Bryce declared that New York, Baltimore, Chicago, and San Francisco "have done their best to poison" their respective legislatures by filling them with "numbers of a low type, as well as being themselves the centers of enormous accumulations of capital." Thus, he charged, the cities combined the strongest corrupting force with the most corruptible material, producing "such a Witches' Sabbath of jobbing, bribing, thieving, and prostitution of legislative power to private interest as the world has seldom seen." He hastened to add, however, that in the states afflicted by large cities, the majority of legislators were

---

[10] Lincoln Steffens, *The Shame of the Cities* (New York: S. S. McClure Co., 1902).

[11] This is not to suggest the absence of antipathy. George Washington Plunkitt, for example, was one of many New York City political leaders who dreamed of separate statehood for the city and condemned the "hayseed"-run state government; ". . . the people here," he declard, "are nothin' but slaves of the Albany gang." William L. Riordan, *Plunkitt of Tammany Hall* (New York: E. P. Dutton & Co., Inc., 1963), pp. 65-66.

not bad men, "for the majority come from the rural districts or smaller towns, where honesty and order reign as they do generally in Northern and Western America outside a few large cities." [12]

Evidence of inferiority was at hand in the state house itself. After the gap in ability and honesty narrowed between rural and urban members, the antipathy remained, often fed by growing minority group representation in the legislature and by divisions over social welfare legislation and government spending practices.

While the basis for an urban-rural conflict existed in many legislatures, its presence tended to be felt only on certain kinds of issues, not on the full range of matters before the legislature. When country and city were competitors in pauperism, seeking priorities in state assistance, the conflict often became real. In some areas of social legislation the division was largely—but by no means exclusively—urban-rural in character. Prohibition, workmen's compensation, assistance to the needy were early sources of urban-rural friction, as were highway priorities and equalization formulas for distribution of state revenues back to local governments.

As the 20th century progressed, and as the acts of legislatures became more issue-oriented, the myth or fear of power loss as the basis for urban-rural cleavage tended to be reinforced by conflict over policy. While the policy debate was colored by ruralism or urbanism, it emphasized a new factor in explaining the persistence of malapportionment. Cities were not homogeneous units, but given the districting and balloting practices for legislative elections, city legislative representation tended to be of one piece, one party, or one faction. Thus a fairly large urban-based group often had no official voice in the legislature. The minority party, the industrialists, bankers, and chambers of commerce frequently found themselves without legislative representatives as a result of the politics of garnering a majority of votes from the city's plural group structure. Those who opposed legal recognition of labor unions, for example, or workmen's compensation laws, made few alliances with city senators or representatives who found their majorities in the working class wards. They often found a ready alliance with rural members, who also opposed such legislation with parochial fervor.

Rural over-representation was clearly advantageous to urban-based interests who saw in reapportionment only the threat of more representation for unionists, low income groups, and ethnic minori-

<hr/>

[12] Bryce, *The American Commonwealth, op. cit.,* pp. 580-581.

ties. In 1948 the California Chamber of Commerce and the Los
Angeles *Times* opposed amendments to the California Constitution which were designed to increase urban representation in the
state senate. The virulent campaign against a population basis for
the legislature succeeded. Even Los Angeles County voted against
the amendment, leading one observer to comment that the campaign and its result "gave meager support for the dogma that man
is a rational being." [13] Some urban interests also supported the
"balanced legislature plan" of representation in Michigan, and
backed an amendment to fix senatorial representation by area.[14]
The general attitude represented by these actions seemed well sum-
marized by *Nation's Business,* house organ of the Chamber of Commerce of the United States, in its reaction to *Baker* v. *Carr:*

> . . . the businessman might suggest [the effects of reapportionment] on
> his own business by asking: "What would have happened, say, to the
> right to work bill in my state if the legislature had been controlled
> by the urban population with its strong, politically active segment of
> organized labor." [15]

A second, less principled and less obvious alliance also developed
between urban-based interests and the country lawmakers. Frequent
financial liaisons developed between firms doing business with the
state and with legislators. The practice of companies' giving lawyer-
legislators retainers is a widespread one. A large industry may offer
every lawyer-member some business, the eventual withdrawal of
which might cause severe economic privations for the member
grown dependent on such largess. Other members become sales representatives for construction firms or agents of insurance companies. Legislators in the insurance business could eventually find
that a sizable portion of their accounts come from firms with an
interest in state legislative or administrative activity. Again, these
accounts often provide substantial increases in income, and the
possibility of their withdrawal for a "wrong" vote, therefore, carries
economic as well as political sanctions.

[13] Gordon E. Baker, "The California Senate: Sectional Conflict and *Vox
Populi*," in Malcolm Jewell, ed., *The Politics of Reapportionment* (New
York: Atherton Press, 1962), p. 52.
[14] At the same time, a population based apportionment failed to be adopted.
See Karl Lamb's report in Jewell, *The Politics of Reapportionment, op. cit.*,
p. 268.
[15] "What Reapportionment Means to You," *Nation's Business* (July 1962), p.
29.

In Florida, for instance, a substantial alliance has been reported between the "pork choppers" who have over-represented rural Florida, and alert entrepreneurs who sought state indulgence to function most profitably.[16] This sort of cozy relationship which technically violated no laws (since few effective conflict of interest laws exist covering state legislators) tended to cut across urban-rural boundaries and operated to restrain any passion for reapportionment on the part of either rural representatives or their occupational benefactors. Tales of defeated or retiring members losing business to their successors in office usually disabuses a member of any illusion that he has been sought out by his political-economic client solely because of his innate ability completely divorced from his official status.

To members so benefiting, reapportionment means, in addition to its unpleasant policy implications, a real possibility of reduced income. While the client could surely approach the new members seated after reapportionment, political receptivity may be different, given a constituency for the new urban member which may have conflicting policy interests to those of the client. Moreover, the risks of destroying tried and true relationships for unsure new arrangements are high enough to encourage tacit, if not overt, disapproval of reapportionment.

Thus, while the urban-rural conflict is a valid explanation underlying the continuation of malapportionment, it is far from being a complete one. The myth of rural superiority, the fear of city domination, and the disagreements over policy for such matters as taxes, distribution of state funds, local government powers, and civil rights tend to be buttressed by a group based political structure which may well have its economic roots in the city but its branches in the over-represented rural districts.

Sectionalism has tended to modify urban-rural cleavage. In California it reached its most pronounced stage in the rivalry for representation between the northern and southern sections of the state. In the older states, there was a reluctance on the part of the settled eastern regions to give up seats to the developing western frontier. Party loyalties also are frequently more important in determining voting behavior than are urban or rural origins. Such factors as these, and even rivalry between large urban centers for a larger share of power—as in the political competition of Cleveland and

<hr />

[16] William C. Harvard and Loren P. Beth, *The Politics of Misrepresentation* (Baton Rouge, La.: Louisiana State University Press, 1962), pp. 24, 34.

Cincinnati, Shreveport and New Orleans, Dallas and Houston, or Philadelphia and Pittsburgh—also mitigated the significance of the urban-rural conflict as an explanation for the denigration of representative government.[17]

As urban expansion continued and clearly changed in character after 1930 to a low density overspill into the suburbs, a complicating factor was added to reapportionment politics. The central cities became more fairly represented as their growth rate stabilized or even declined while that of the suburbs soared. The suburbs became increasingly victims of malapportionment, but at first the victims did not seem to mind too much. The suburbs were in one sense "anti-urbs," reactions against the social and political life of the city. While an integral part of the urban complex, the suburbs in their early stages of growth were often more likely to be politically allied with rural forces than with the core cities. Thus, the urban population was not of one mind on the question of reapportionment. As the suburban boom continued, however, the suburbs began to develop an awareness of their distinctive needs and of the necessity for more representation in the legislature to achieve them. By the time they had become aware of their "unbanness"—their political distinction from the rural population—the city politicians who had long provided the basic support for whatever reapportionment effort there was began to lose interest in the subject. Reapportionment now meant little or no gain in central city seats; in some cases it would result in a loss of power in both relative and absolute terms.

A few examples suggest how radical was the shift in potential power from 1930 to 1960. In 1930 New York City had only seventy-one per cent of its population's share of legislative representation, but in 1960, it had ninety-three per cent of the representation to which its population was entitled. By contrast, suburban counties had gone from a status of overrepresentation to one of under-representation. In 1930 the vote of a citizen of Baltimore was worth only fifty-one per cent of its fair value, but without any change in representation for the city and even with modest increases in representation outside the city in the interim, the same Baltimorean's vote in 1960 was eighty-three per cent as good as it should have been. The Maryland suburbs suffered a shocking decline of position, however.

[17] For a useful discussion of voting blocs in state legislatures, see Malcolm E. Jewell, *The State Legislature: Politics and Practice* (New York: Random House, 1962), chap. 3, pp. 48-76.

In Baltimore County, which is legally separate from the city, a vote's value declined in the thirty years from fifty-five to twenty-six per cent of parity, and in Montgomery County in the Washington, D.C. suburbs, it fell from 134 per cent to thirty-eight per cent of parity.[18] Of the twenty-three counties throughout the nation in 1960 in which the value of the vote was less than half of its fair value, only four were "central city" counties; the remainder were suburban.[19]

As this trend became clear, city representatives were less willing than before to support reapportionment. Ironically, with the spread of population to new areas of the states, the chances of passing a reasonable reapportionment act diminished. Central city legislators saw nothing to gain by adding to suburban legislative strength.[20] This would mean no more votes and perhaps even less legislative strength in fighting for more funds for the core city, redevelopment legislation, metropolitan service districts, and other urban projects under city leadership. Rural over-representation, often buttressed by a partisan division between urban and rural areas, remained the "reason" the city could not get its fair share from the state, but now reapportionment was not the panacea it once had seemed to the city politicians.[21]

In some cases, then, the struggle for political supremacy between city and suburbs overlay the traditional urban-rural conflict. The hard core of opposition to change remained in the provinces, but the proponents of change grew weaker rather than stronger as their statistical numbers increased. Moreover, the years of malapportionment had produced a set of myths to support legislative practice. The referendums in California and Michigan suggested that these myths had such a hold on the population that proposals to limit urban representation could carry even the cities. Compounded of

[18] For a full presentation of these and other population figures, see Paul T. David and Ralph Eisenberg, *Devaluation of the Urban and Suburban Vote* (Charlottesville, Va.: University of Virginia Press, 1961), pp. 12-13.
[19] *Ibid.*, p. 14.
[20] Maryland is a good case in point. In 1960 it became apparent that in another ten years Baltimore, due to its slow growth in comparison with the suburbs, would be overrepresented. In the reapportionment battle in that state, the principal concern of the Baltimore City delegation was the development of a formula which would guarantee the city against a loss of seats.
[21] See Robert L. Friedman, "The Urban-Rural Conflict Revisited," *Western Political Quarterly*, XIV (1961), 483.

the traditional agrarian ideal, fear and distaste for the city and its organized politics, interest groups, and intra-urban disagreements, there developed the doctrine of "balanced representation," which could be used as justification for the system or as a polite answer to the reformer.

The idea and the laws which announced it were not motivated by the force of the thought alone. It was primarily a convenient façade to hide the bald face of indifferent or intransigent power, but the idea fed back on its protagonists. The idea of balanced representation lost its origin in antiquity and became an article of belief reinforcing political instinct.

The Legislative Character

This close look at the myth and reality of the urban-rural conflict provides only one ingredient in explaining the impasse: the major external factor. To understand fully the problem, it is necessary to examine the internal relations of the legislature.

Of all the popularly chosen bodies in the United States, none is probably as poorly studied, poorly reported, and poorly understood as the state legislature. From its grand beginning as antagonist of the colonial governor, it has declined to a low status among governmental institutions. It is endured, it sometimes seems, only because no one has invented a substitute. The political standing of its members is usually so low that most of them, unless notorious for colorful mannerisms or unsavory involvements, are almost invisible players in the game of politics. "The prestige of a member of this House," an Oklahoma state representative once lamented to a colleague, "is about as high as the piano player in a whore house."

This unflattering self-assessment is reflected in public attitudes toward the state legislature. A 1963 poll of Albuquerque, New Mexico citizens sought opinions on the performance of the state legislature, Congress, the city's public schools, and commercial television. Eighty two per cent approved of the school's performance, sixty-six per cent of television, and sixty-four per cent of Congress. But only forty-two per cent of the respondents approved the performance of the state legislature. The poll, taken since 1955, has consistently reflected lower opinions of the legislature than of the school system, the Congress, or even commercial television. The opinion pollster reported:

> Over a period of time it is apparent that about one out of ten Albuquerqueans thinks the New Mexico legislature does a good job; in contrast, almost two out of three Albuquerqueans think that the New Mexico legislature does a bad job or are so disinterested in the legislature that they express no opinion.[22]

Undoubtedly, as V. O. Key, Jr. has pointed out, many factors conspired to produce the low status of the legislature and its members.

> Yet, among these factors, its unrepresentative character must be assigned a high rank. A body that often acts reluctantly under executive pressure and whose chief purpose often seems to be one only of negation cannot but in the long run lose prestige.[23]

The state legislator normally is underpaid, works at legislating at a financial sacrifice, and gets little thanks for his work. Usually he has no staff, shares a secretary with a dozen other members, and depends for bill drafting on the overworked legislative council staff, lobbyists, lawyer friends, or local government attorneys. Many able people somehow find time to serve, but it is important to remember that in spite of the popular notion that legislatures are excellent training ground for Congress and the governorship, only a few are so trained.

For the overwhelming majority of its members, the legislature is the end of the political road; the highest office ever held or sought. This in itself tends to impose a limitation of perspective and concept of the representative role. It may not be as a Maryland delegate said of his colleagues, "They don't know why they are here." Many know why they are there, and stay there by expressing highly parochial sentiments and securing their fair share of the goods and services the state has to distribute to constituents. Their reputations, small measured by statewide or congressional standards, are often monumental in the home precincts.

The objective of legislative service, when it is not to further ambition for a higher office, is to broaden one's influence in the legislature itself and in the state. An effective legislator is not neces-

[22] Frederick C. Irion, "Alberquerque Opinion, 1963," unpublished memorandum, August 26, 1963.
[23] V. O. Key, Jr., *American State Politics: An Introduction* (New York: Alfred A. Knopf, Inc., 1956), pp. 76-77.

sarily an able one by standards that political scientists might establish, but then few political scientists have a working knowledge of
the exigencies of legislative politics. And few legislators know or
care what the political scientists think. The former are artisans in
politics, and they respond to the master artisan. The man who gets
things done understands the system, his colleagues' interests and
reactions, and feels the pulse of an often disorganized, if not plainly
disorderly, gaggle of petty politicians.

The basic concern of many members and often of the leadership is
less the substance of legislation than the appearance of legislating.
A man too highly committed to the content of laws saps his effectiveness by being unable to barter freely among his colleagues and the
lobbyists. Content of legislation has tended increasingly to be the
special province first of the administration, and second, the lobbyists.
Only the exceptional member has the time and resources to act in
his own behalf in shaping any major legislation. Most are dependent
on the leadership, voting loyally their support in return for the
group benefits which the leaders control: internal status through
committee assignments, patronage, and "little kindnesses," such as
being picked as author for important bills, appointment to the
Legislative Council or to interstate organizations or conferences.

The legislature is a social group. Understanding this is vital to
understanding its reaction to an anti-group invention like reapportionment. It tends to be socially cohesive in spite of its complex
political makeup. It tends to be collectively defensive of its prerogatives, its leaders, and its reputation. Scarcely a session passes but
that a number of members take the floor to denounce the press for
its poor or biased reporting of the legislature, thus giving it a "bad
image" before the public. This *esprit de corps* is usually divisible
by houses, and an intrusion of one house upon the affairs of the
other or the impediment of perquisites by "the other body" may
also occasion histrionic outbursts. A member indicted by a grand
jury may be given a vote of confidence or at least a round of ap-
plause to cheer him up. Being a legislator is special, and to the
members their house takes on many attributes of a fraternal order.

Success in the order depends on mastery of the ritual, the incan-
tations, and the norms of behavior. Such a system is well hedged
against change. A member soon learns to "get along by going along."
Unlike Congress, seniority alone does not guarantee status in most
legislatures, but legislative creativity and competence are rarely the

prime factors either. Pursuit of the main chance is a surer road to a committee chair or leadership position. This involves cultivation of both internal and external political fields. Support of the right candidate for governor is often a crucial factor. Gubernatorial support can frequently overcome any hindrance to advancement. Power is distributed in the legislature more by design than chance. Proper party and factional alignment is important. A degree of team play is essential to maintain one's position in the legislature.

An alternative route to power is to act as a spokesman for an outside group—retailers, farmers, labor, teachers, or even inmates of the state penitentiary. With good group liaison and with the expenditure of a little time, a member can become the recognized authority for his house, and if not on the subject matter, then at least on the temper or attitude of his group. This special interest may frequently lead to a committee chair won through pressures applied both inside and outside the legislature.

In addition to the leaders of the order, there are also "vetoers" in the legislature—members of a lesser rank and lobbyists who may not be able to lead, but who speak so clearly or intently for their special causes that the general spirit of accommodation permits elimination of clauses offensive to their interests.[24] Local delegations frequently can prevent legislation harmful to their jurisdiction. Moreover, a comity prevails among members in regard to special and local legislation. So long as its effect is limited to the area or interest represented by a member, his desire to pass the legislation is usually its passport through the legislature.

It is into this milieu that legislation is thrust. The volume of bills alone demands a system of priorities. In the legislature this is a dual system—that of the administration and leadership, and that of the individual members.

The governor sets the basic priority system. He is guided by what the state agencies demand, his own predispositions, and an assessment of what the legislature can accomplish in the limited time it will meet. In general, an item such as reapportionment tends to have low legislative priority. It is the one issue which tears at the

---

[24] Occasionally a lobbyist may become exceedingly powerful and share widely in the exercise of legislative power. Artie Samish developed such a reputation in California, as did George Hocker in Maryland. Both lobbied for liquor or beer industries. For a discussion of the role of Samish see Lester Velie, "The Secret Boss of California," *Collier Magazine* (August 13, 1949).

base of the legislative order. It not only is a source of division among the members; it strikes at the distribution of power within and outside the legislature, and it poses a threat to specific members of the legislative group.

Because the issue is so divisive, and because it threatens a working coalition with bitter personal discord, reapportionment has high priority only as a campaign issue for the governor. If he introduces it into the legislature, it is likely that he and his leaders will program it for consideration after other major business has been disposed of or at a special session.[25]

Moreover, since reapportionment so directly affects the legislature as an institution, handling the matter is often a jealously guarded legislative prerogative. If a governor is active at all he often is in the role of a stern father giving advice. More frequently, governors are passive participants, waiting for the legislature to produce something.[26] A few governors, like Leroy Collins of Florida and J. Howard Edmondson of Oklahoma, took vigorous stands on reapportionment. The results were not such as would encourage the spread of the practice to other chief executives. The Florida legislature produced a meager change which was rejected by the voters, and the Oklahoma legislature virtually ignored the governor. The expenditure of gubernatorial influence required to maneuver a reapportionment bill through the legislature was too great to expend on one issue with so little chance of success. In the words of Governor David L. Lawrence of Pennsylvania, "The first job of the governor is to govern." He cannot govern with a hostile legislature.

From the point of view of the legislator—even the urban member —reapportionment also tended to have low priority. The chances for passage were usually remote. If the issue were pressed vigorously, friends were bound to be alienated as they fought for their political survival. This would endanger other goals which were obtainable— local or functional legislation. For the most part, avid sponsorship of reapportionment measures entailed all risk and no reward. Why should the legislator make a nuisance of himself on so futile a project?

[25] For an example, see Gordon E. Baker, *The Politics of Reapportionment in Washington* (New York: Holt, Rinehart & Winston, Inc., 1960).
[26] Jewell, *The Politics of Reapportionment, op. cit.,* p. 31.

The Psychology of the Issue

In the legislative environment, the reapportionment issue is stripped of its public importance and ideological base. It becomes instead a private settlement among the members. At best it is a painful experience. It means unseating colleagues without the benefit of an election for the people who had formerly elected them. It means the cynical employment of partisan calculus in the new distribution of seats. "Arrangement" better describes the process than "apportionment."

In addition to the club-dissolving problems and internal status problems discussed above, the urban member also frequently has other strains on his ability to espouse reapportionment. To illustrate the point, consider the case of a composite member whose characteristics are drawn from interviews, observation, and the literature: a state senator from a suburban county.

The senator is the central political figure in his sprawling county. As the sole senator from the county, his power rests on his absolute prerogative to promote or kill local legislation and his extensive control over state patronage for the county. Election judges, road workers, prison guards, statehouse employees, game wardens, commissioners of state-appointed authorities, and the local automobile license tag agent—all depend on him for their positions. Reapportionment would mean sharing that power and a major reduction in his influence. It would open opportunities to party and factional rivals, especially if legislative districts are created for each senator rather than providing for elections at large. Senatorial districts could even end his political career. As a Republican, he lives in an area sure to become a Democratic district. He can easily envision the political problems which reapportionment will bring him. "Can't you just see seven senators from this county agreeing on the tag agent?"

Practical political consideration may outweigh the Senator's commitment "in principle" to reapportionment. He would certainly introduce legislation of a "practical" nature, perhaps adding a few seats in the house, but leaving the senate untouched— a recognition of senatorial belief in the analogy of the state senate's non-population base to that of the U.S. Senate. Such a bill is reasonably safe. It makes a record without damaging his legislative reputation as a practical and realistic senator.

The problems of the rural member are far simpler. He has no real inner conflicts. He opposes reapportionment. He also is acutely aware of the extent of hypocrisy practiced by members such as the suburban senator. His fear is of members—non-club types—sincere in their objective of reapportionment and willing to upset the house and even electoral politics on the gubernatorial level to achieve it. But the rural member reflects many of the fears and myths discussed earlier. He not only sees his seat in the legislature in danger but probably believes in the myth of agrarian superiority. He senses danger to "conservatism" as he defines it through an increase in urban power. That the suburbs would be the primary beneficiaries of reapportionment does not mean anything different to him. It might even be worse, since there is a danger that new suburban representatives of his party will change its character—even its leadership—in the legislature. He is genuinely afraid that new urban interests will run roughshod over rural interests.

He knows the legislature. He knows its members. He knows the power system and he knows that if he and his colleagues from the sparsely populated areas stand firm against any change, they have the power to prevent one. Even when convinced that change is inevitable, his instinct is to resist it altogether. Compromise is unthinkable unless it is absolutely necessary. Both he and the suburban senator count on retaining the status quo because they both believe the issue is not a basic one in public cognizance. "The yokels hang on," Mencken might well have said, "because nobody cares very much."

But sometimes people do care. The League of Women Voters of Washington succeeded in forcing a reapportionment through the initiative and referendum process. The legislature reacted to its prospective reapportionment by amending the referendum to dilute its effect: to provide a better arrangement for the members.[27] "You'll not tell us what to do—we'll tell you," a rural delegate told the vice-president of the Maryland Committee for Fair Representation at a hearing on reapportionment.

The rural member can, if he must, resort to tactics which will invariably temper the result, if not forestall it altogether. He can propose legislative districts; he can quibble over boundaries; he

[27] Baker, *The Politics of Reapportionment in Washington.*

can, if all else fails, filibuster the rules. For the most part he is annoyed but is sure of success. If in real danger of defeat, he may of course become desperate.

Desperation is itself a good defense in the legislative environment. It tends to excite sympathy and encourage accommodation from other members in order to prevent disruption of the equilibrium of the legislature. Rural desperation, an urban member's hypocrisy, and the eternal problem of securing the required majority of votes to pass the new arrangement provide the basis for what appear to be the unwritten rules of legislative reapportionment. As such, the factors mentioned above help explain the lack of substantial change which has contributed almost as much to the decline of representative government as has the outright failure of the legislature to act on apportionment.

The general rule is "the least loss to the least number." Within this dictum are the following clearly discernible patterns:

1. *Save the incumbents.* Where districts must be combined or divided, the first rule is so to arrange the boundaries that the incumbents who wish to run again are assured a district. If an old district must be divided, the division is accomplished in a manner giving the incumbent the most favorable district possible. All incumbents, of course, cannot always be saved. In some cases, their places of residence necessitate that two incumbents must oppose each other for a single seat. This leads to other rules.

2. *Cut the retirees.* Wherever possible, the district of a retiring member will be combined with that of another incumbent. Of course, it must be understood that the combination itself may accelerate certain other retirements.

3. *Cut the minority party.* If incumbents must oppose each other, an attempt will be made to combine districts held by members of the minority party or districts held by different parties rather than majority districts.

4. *Increase the size of the house in preference to reapportioning.* Unless restricted by the state constitution, this affords the most painless method of adjustment. Members and/or districts are simply added to the quota of the largest jurisdictions while no representation is reduced in any area. This insures a slower relative loss of power than if the existing seats were redistributed.

5. *To each his own.* The rule has a double meaning. First it suggests that each house should handle separately its own apportionment problem and that the other should accept the result

without substantial change. The basic public question of representation is thereby enveloped in the more club-like concept of *membership*. Each club is the best judge of its own members. The second meaning of the rule is that each boundary problem should be settled by the delegation directly concerned. Thus, in Illinois, the Cook County delegation worked out the district boundaries in the county, and the legislature accepted their decision.[28] In Maryland, redistricting of Baltimore city was a matter left entirely to the discretion of the city's delegation.

6. *Compensate in one house for any concessions in the other.* If reapportionment is politically or constitutionally unavoidable, make all concessions in one house, and invoke the "balanced government" concept to reduce or at least fix at the present level the representation of areas benefiting in the first house. This can be done by the use of a little "federal plan" or by the use of other discriminatory formulas for assignment of seats. When a legislative group holds absolute power to reapportion, it can usually extract a high price for its consent to any plan apportioning one house on a more popular basis. That price is frequently a compensating increase in minority power in the other house, or at best leaving it untouched.[29]

THE POLITICS
OF A SPECIFIC PLAN

The almost pure political consideration of the unwritten rules indicates the seriousness of the problem facing the legislator or citizen urging reapportionment. There has been an almost all pervasive absence of accepted standards for fair representation. State constitutions, of course, contained some requirements, but often these could be met explicitly and malapportionment still prevailed. In some cases the constitutional standards themselves

---

[28] Gilbert Y. Steiner and Samuel K. Gove, *Legislative Politics in Illinois* (Urbana, Ill.: University of Illinois Press, 1960), pp. 97ff.
[29] The California and Michigan experiences were mentioned above. Illinois was divided into "areas" of apportionment to prevent Cook County supremacy. See Steiner and Gove, *Legislative Politics, op. cit.*, p. 85. In 1946 the New Jersey Legislature which called a constitutional convention specified in the call that the allocation of one senator to each county should not be disturbed.

were deliberate means of discrimination against urban areas or political parties.[30]

Where a change in the apportionment system would change a party's control in the legislature, it was doubly resisted. In states like New York, Michigan, Pennsylvania, New Jersey, Connecticut, Indiana, Illinois, and California, any major change toward fairness based on population standards would also endanger the historic control of one or both houses by the incumbent political party. In Maryland and Texas, party revolution would probably not have resulted, but a change in the prevailing distribution of seats between the parties would most certainly occur.

The status quo in such states guaranteed government divided between the parties. Whatever their majorities, governors in some states could anticipate the partisan opposition of at least one house of the legislature. Through his twelve years as governor, G. Mennen Williams never succeeded in electing a Democratic senate, and through eight years of dominance of state politics in Maryland, Governor Theodore R. McKeldin, Jr., had no hope for a Republican legislature. The result of this partisan division on state policy was often stalemated government. Partisan separation of interest when added to constitutional separation of powers brought Michigan almost to the verge of bankruptcy as the governor and the senate continued to disagree on tax policy for the state. This led a wag to comment that the system resulted in too many checks and no balance.

In such an environment, a specific plan of apportionment cannot be treated as an abstract principle. The campaign orator's exaltation of the two-party system does not extend to helping the other party. In fact, existing plans (or non-plans) of apportionment were frequently convenient means of suppressing the power of the minority party. Where there is no hope of victory, there is often an atrophy of minority party organization.[31] More representation for cities or suburbs clearly could endanger the party balance. Where seats were to be added, plans have usually been written to minimize gains for the minority party or minority groups, but the "best" solution to the problem was to make no change at all.

Political scientists have dabbled with the apportionment ques-

[30] New York, for example, has often been described as "constitutionally Republican." The same state placed a limitation on the proportion of senators any county might receive.
[31] Key, *American State Politics, op. cit.,* pp. 171ff.

tion for years, but their standards of fairness rarely were written into reapportionment amendments.[32] There was some evidence of consensus among experts regarding generalities about fairness, but there was an almost equal consensus among legislators to ignore any such standards. The critical deficiency was that whatever standards were in the public domain, none were selected as official and binding on the behavior of the legislatures. This absence of standards led quite naturally to a completely *ad hoc* approach to an arrangement of seats. Existing disparities were allowed to remain while others might be remedied. In Maryland representation was frozen at its 1940 distribution to prevent small counties from gaining more seats. In Delaware there was no means short of constitutional amendment for changing the apportionment. In some states no action at all was taken. Tennessee and Alabama had last apportioned in 1901, Oklahoma in 1907. In other states, seats were added to the most underrepresented areas—usually a token increase.

Apportionment, then, either did not occur at all, or was determined by practices more common to horse trading than to political theory. Unwanted areas were shuffled off on minority members or divided to prevent a growing voice for an "outside" group. Thus a city might be redistricted to prevent a gain in Negro voting strength from being reflected in the legislature. It was not uncommon for representatives from overpopulated districts to reject certain kinds of reapportionment measures. Malapportionment was preferred to a boundary adjustment which would reduce the plurality of the incumbent, or even invite competition from the minority party in the district. In developing a specific plan of apportionment in a political atmosphere devoid of compulsory minimum standards of fairness, the power to act or assent was frequently used irresponsibly by all concerned, urban as well as rural members.

"We come as beggars," an urban representative said in urging the legislature to reapportion itself with an eye toward greater equity. But beggars could not be choosers. The internal power and value system of the legislatures would not yield. As the population grew and expanded outward, legislative power became even more remotely related to electoral strength and irresponsibility increased, for the impact of a fair reapportionment would mean ever greater dislocations of the powerful. The harsh fact of life in reapportion-

[32] Standards were formulated, for example, by the American Political Science Association's Committee on Legislatures. See Belle Zeller, ed., *American State Legislatures* (New York: Thomas Y. Crowell Co., 1954), p. 46.

ment politics was that the necessary votes were not available for a respectable bill—and often not for any bill—and the by-products and practices of the system reinforced its perpetuation. Change became progressively more difficult. It might be said of the state legislatures as it was of the Bourbons of the Old Regime: *Plus ca change, plus c'est la même chose.*

THE COURTS ENTER THE THICKET

Courts ought not to enter this political thicket. The remedy for unfairness in districting is to secure State legislators that will apportion properly, or to invoke the ample powers of Congress.

Mr. Justice Felix Frankfurter
Colegrove v. *Green,* 1946

It is well for this Court to practice self-restraint and discipline in constitutional adjudication, but never in its history have those principles received sanction where the national rights of so many have been so clearly infringed for so long a time.

Mr. Justice Tom Clark
Baker v. *Carr,* 1962

For all practical purposes, the normal avenues for political change of the representative structure were blocked. Almost every attempt at legislative action had been rebuffed. The initiative and referendum were not available as instruments of change in more than thirty states. Where they existed, results were discouraging and always costly for the ordinary citizens group trying to use them to obtain a reapportionment. In the American system of constitutional adjustment, the only remaining route to orderly change lay through the court system.

"Scarcely any political question arises in the United States which is not resolved, sooner or later, into a judicial question," Tocqueville had observed in 1837.[1] It is one thing to observe a condition as Tocqueville had. But it is quite another to produce such a condition. Courts operate under their own rules. If a political change

[1] Alexis de Tocqueville, *Democracy in America,* I (New York: Vintage Press, 1945).

is to be wrought through the agency of the judiciary, the problem must be framed in a way that permits a court to handle it, and to dispose of it. American courts do not, as a rule, decide abstract questions. A real controversy and a real injury normally are required to raise an issue which the courts will choose to decide.

A second basic element is also involved in a federal system. If a law case is to have national scope, it must be decided by the Supreme Court of the United States. Otherwise all states, and even all federal judicial circuits, are not bound. Some state courts clearly had decided apportionment cases, but their opinions were usually limited to enforcement of the state constitution. If that document was biased against equality, a state court decision based on it was of little value even in a single state, much less the nation.

In order to otain a ruling from the Supreme Court of the United States the case must present a "federal" question arising under the U.S. Constitution or the federal laws. An apportionment case does not arise under the Supreme Court's original jurisdiction.[2] It must reach the court on appeal from a state's highest court or by writ of certiorari from a lower federal court. Given the existing state apportionment practices and constitutional provisions, a suitable argument had to be developed to support a theory of federal constitutional protection for representation based on population.

Moreover, those seeking judicial relief must demonstrate to the courts that the fair representation issue was not only a federal constitutional question, but a question which the courts could legally and constitutionally decide. Courts maintain considerable discretion in determining which equity cases they will decide.[3] While a valid issue is frequently presented, a court may have the option of deciding that the most judicious disposition of the case is not to decide it at all. This may result from an assessment of the damage which might result from a decision, or because the case is brought at such a time that a decision might cause greater hardship than a

---

[2] The original jurisdiction of the Supreme Court extends only to cases between the federal government and one of the states, between two or more states, to cases involving ambassadors and foreign officials, and suits initiated by a state against a citizen of another state, an alien, or a foreign government.

[3] Equity is a supplement to the common law. Cases in equity take the form of a judicial decree, not a judgment of "yes" or "no." Equity allows the judge to use preventive means, such as injunction, to assure the result he decrees, or even to fashion a relief which he believes appropriate to the case, and then to enjoin interference with the order.

refusal to decide. Finally, the courts usually decline to decide those cases which they class as "political questions." These are controversies which the courts have held to be the prerogatives of the legislative or executive branches of the government. A "political question" may also be one in which it is difficult or impossible for the courts to devise rules or standards which they can manage through normal judicial procedures. The Supreme Court, for instance, has refused under the political question doctrine to decide whether a state has a republican form of government.[4] Likewise, it has declined to provide judicial enforcement for the second section of the Fourteenth Amendment,[5] and has declined to define the war powers of the President of the United States.[6] The problem in legal strategy, then, was twofold. A litigant must demonstrate not only that the court *could* decide the question but that it is a question which *should* be decided by the court.

These are not simply abstract questions. A judicial decision has consequences in the real world. In matters such as reapportionment, if a case is brought by a single citizen, a decision for either side affects not just the rights of the single citizen but the rights and power of every other citizen in the state. Also, a court in making a decision wishes to see it take effect. Consequently courts are reluctant to announce rulings which cannot be implemented. Normally the power to issue injunctions and writs of mandamus or citations of contempt are sufficient to guarantee compliance with the relief the court orders in a case. But normally these powers are exercised against individuals or officials who have the authority to perform the acts required by the court. Legislatures, however, generally possess the power to apportion. And courts have rarely, if ever, issued a writ of mandamus against a legislature, enjoined it from acting, or held a legislature to be in contempt of court. There is no practical way to enforce such orders. A legislative majority can hardly be jailed because it fails to agree with a court's ruling. Thus the courts had to be convinced not only that they could and must decide, but that their decisions could be implemented. This meant finding defendants with power to act whom the court could enjoin, require to act, or hold in contempt of court in order to extract compliance. Finally, the courts must be reasonably certain that if all else failed they could fashion a suitable relief—in this instance,

[4] *Luther* v. *Borden,* 7 How. 1 (1849).
[5] *Sanders* v. *Wilkins,* 329 U.S. 825 (1946).
[6] *Curtiss-Wright Export Corp.* v. *U.S.,* 299 U.S. 304 (1936).

actually reapportion a state—and enjoin the appropriate officials from interfering with implementation of such a decree.[7]

Meeting these problems involved, in turn, the development of legal standards for fair representation, satisfaction of certain legal and political conditions to justify bringing a case to court, and reaching the appropriate court at the proper time with the requisite set of facts and arguments.

THE FIRST ASSAULT:
Colegrove v. Green

In 1946, political scientist Kenneth Colegrove of Northwestern University made the first assault on the constitutionality of unequal representation.[8] In a complaint filed in federal district court in Chicago, he argued that as a resident of the Seventh Congressional District of Illinois, he was deprived of his constitutional right to equal protection of the laws under the Fourteenth Amendment to the U.S. Constitution. The Seventh District contained over 900,000 people, while the Fifth District contained a little more than 100,000. Colegrove maintained that this disparity in populations meant his vote was worth only one-eighth that of a resident of the Fifth District.

Colegrove's suit was dismissed by a three judge federal court, from which he appealed to the Supreme Court. That tribunal also dismissed his suit, but only after dividing sharply on the question of jurisdiction to try the case. The case was decided after the death of Chief Justice Stone, who had heard the argument and participated in the initial conference on the case. The new chief justice, Fred Vinson, had not yet taken office when the decision was announced. Mr. Justice Robert Jackson did not participate in the case because he was in Nuremberg as chief U.S. prosecutor at the Nazi war crimes trials. Thus only seven members of the court were available to make the decision. Mr. Justice Frankfurter wrote an opinion which dismissed the complaint, but also held the whole matter of the apportionment of legislative or congressional representation to be a "political question." He was joined by two other justices in his view that

[7] Alfred L. Scanlan, "Problems of Pleading, Proof and Persuasion in a Reapportionment Case," 38 Notre Dame Lawyer 420 (June 1963).
[8] Colegrove v. Green, 328 U.S. 549 (1946).

. . . The petitioners ask of this Court what is beyond its competence to grant . . . because due regard for the effective working of our government revealed this issue to be of a peculiarly political nature and therefore not meet for judicial determination.[9]

Mr. Justice Wiley Rutledge wrote a separate opinion concurring in the dismissal, but basing his decision on equity grounds. The case had been brought before the Supreme Court for argument only a month before the Illinois primary elections. By the time it was decided the primary had already been held. Rutledge objected to upsetting the 1946 election process at a stage when nominees had already been chosen for existing districts. He did not agree with the Frankfurter opinion's assertion, however, that the matter was a political question over which the federal courts lacked jurisdiction.[10] Mr. Justice Hugo Black joined by Justices William Douglas and Frank Murphy strongly dissented. Black argued that districting was no more political than the voting rights cases decided by the court.[11] He felt the court not only had jurisdiction under the Equal Protection Clause, but also that it should have decided the case in favor of Professor Colegrove, by enjoining the elections unless held at large or on the basis of districts equal in population.[12]

Colegrove illustrates the problems of framing a political issue in legal terms. It also illustrates the hazards of resolving such issues through legal procedures as well as the difficulties in finding the legal rules for a decision issuing from a deeply divided court. Analysis of these problems helps explain the decision, its aftermath, and its impact upon subsequent legal strategy and tactics.

One of the principal problems in *Colegrove* v. *Green* was the ease with which the political question doctrine could be invoked. While other congressional districting cases and similar types of electoral problems had been decided by the court,[13] none raised the basic constitutional issue of Equal Protection. Only statutory interpretations had been required. Moreover, since the case dealt with congressional districts, it was clear that Congress itself could act under Article I of the Constitution to correct the problem. Congress had, until 1929, required reasonable equality of popula-

[9] 328 U.S. 549, 552.
[10] 328 U.S. 549, 564, Mr. Justice Rutledge, concurring.
[11] 328 U.S. 549, 569, Mr. Justice Black, dissenting.
[12] 328 U.S. 549, 574.
[13] *Smiley* v. *Holm,* 285 U.S. 355 (1932); *Koenig* v. *Flynn,* 285 U.S. 375 (1932); *Carroll* v. *Becker,* 285 U.S. 380 (1932); *Wood* v. *Broom,* 287 U.S. 1 (1932).

tion among districts. The equality section of the federal redistricting law was abandoned at that time, however. It could easily be
argued, therefore, as Mr. Justice Frankfurter did, that the proper
relief was not through the court, but through the Congress.[14]

While it was true that the districting act was a state law and
apparently subject to the limitations on state action imposed by the
Fourteenth Amendment, Professor Colegrove could appeal to Congress for a remedy if the legislature would not act. The legislature
had not acted contrary to federal law—an expression by Congress
of its will in this area. Colegrove could not, under these circumstances, demonstrate that all other remedies had truly been exhausted and that only the Court remained. Justice Frankfurter and
his colleagues felt the professor was trying to get from the Court
what he had failed to get, or even failed to ask, of the legislature—
the branch of government with clear power to correct the problem.

Secondly, the timing of the suit was poor. It commenced only
after the election process had begun in the existing districts. Candidates had already been nominated in each district by the time the
Supreme Court reached its decision. The state of Illinois as defend-
ant was encouraged to use the doctrine of equitable restraint as a
defense. This argument was conclusive for Mr. Justice Rutledge,
who was unwilling to enter such an involved case so near the election. From another aspect of timing and of propriety he was also
apprehensive of the wisdom of deciding such a case. The Court had
emerged only a few years before from bitter attacks on its propensity
to substitute its judgments for those of legislatures.[15] All but one
of the members voting on the *Colegrove* case had been appointed
by President Franklin D. Roosevelt, who had assailed the "Nine
Old Men" and sought curtailment of the "judicial activism" which
had overturned New Deal legislation. Mr. Justice Frankfurter, a
disciple of the late Justice Oliver Wendell Holmes, was fast becoming the high court's high priest of judicial self-restraint.

The legal meaning of *Colegrove* was not immediately clear from
the conflicting opinions. Did it mean that legislative representation
presented a political question which courts might not decide, or did
it mean only that courts would decline to decide such questions in
similar circumstances on equitable grounds (rather than on the
grounds that they did not possess jurisdiction over the issue)? Did

[14] 328 U.S. 549, 556.
[15] 328 U.S. 549, 564, Mr. Justice Rutledge, concurring.

it mean that the Equal Protection Clause gave no jurisdiction in such cases?

Whatever the confusion surrounding the legal issues of the case, its practical consequences were clear. Illinois' congressional districts had been left standing as before. Technically the court had refused to decide, but it had in fact decided in favor of one of the litigants.

A further practical effect of *Colegrove* soon became obvious: courts, whatever the reasons, were not going to consider representation cases. In 1947, the Supreme Court refused to hear Professor Colegrove's suit challenging the apportionment of the Illinois legislature. In a memorandum order citing the 1946 case, it dismissed his petition for writ of certiorari.[16]

In the next sixteen years, the Court rebuffed eleven attempts to persuade it to hear argument on reapportionment cases.[17] Each time, *Colegrove* was cited as a precedent in memorandum orders dismissing the petition. It was widely assumed that this meant the Court had accepted the Frankfurter opinion as law.[18] State courts as well as federal courts turned away suits, most of the time citing *Colegrove*.[19]

As a decision on the political meaning of the Constitution, *Colegrove* gave sustenance to malapportioned legislatures. Given the political condition and psychology of the legislatures, *Colegrove* reinforced the disinclination of entrenched legislators to reapportion themselves, or to alter congressional district boundaries to accommodate population changes. The political question doctrine, in effect, required courts to decide in favor of the legislative practice of refusing to reapportion and in favor of those benefiting from malapportionment. Constitutional safety reinforced the raw power of incumbent legislators.

[16] *Colegrove* v. *Barnett*, 330 U.S. 804 (1947).

[17] *Cook* v. *Fortson*, 329 U.S. 675 (1946); *Truman* v. *Duckworth*, 329 U.S. 675 (1946); *Colegrove* v. *Barnett*, 330 U.S. 804 (1947); *Tedesso* v. *Bd. of Supervisors of Elections*, 339 U.S. 940 (1950); *Remmey* v. *Smith*, 342 U.S. 916 (1952); *Cox* v. *Peters*, 342 U.S. 936 (1952); *Anderson* v. *Jordan*, 343 U.S. 912 (1952); *Kidd* v. *McCanless*, 352 U.S. 920 (1956); *Radford* v. *Gary*, 352 U.S. 991 (1957); *Hartsfield* v. *Sloan*, 357 U.S. 916 (1958); *Matthews* v. *Handley*, 361 U.S. 127 (1959).

[18] Thomas I. Emerson and David Haber, *Political and Civil Rights in the United States* (Buffalo, N.Y.: Dennis & Co., Inc., 1958), I, 243.

[19] See Robert G. Dixon, Jr., "Legislative Apportionment and the Federal Constitution," 27 *Law and Contemporary Problems* 329, 331-47 (Summer 1962).

THE WEAKENING OF *Colegrove*

The 1950 census showed great shifts in population, but very few
state legislatures acted to reapportion or redistrict, feeling secure
in *Colegrove's* political question doctrine and its implication that
the courts could not interfere. As understanding of the political and
legislative effects of malapportionment grew, *Colegrove* came under
increasing attack, even though no lawsuit seemed capable of overturning it. Appellants could not obtain a hearing before the Supreme Court. Under its rules the Court will hear a case only if
four justices agree to do so. Through the 1950's only three, at most,
apparently wanted to hear argument on any of the cases which
were seeking to challenge the authority of *Colegrove.*

The attack on *Colegrove* was mounted largely by the law reviews.
Between 1950 and 1959, a series of articles critical of the Frankfurter opinion were published.[20] The most influential of these
appeared in the *Harvard Law Review* in 1958. Written by Anthony
Lewis, the Supreme Court correspondent for the *New York Times,*[21]
the article presented a frontal assault on the political question
doctrine as applied to legislative reapportionment and redistricting
cases. Lewis marshaled precedents to show that many state courts
had experienced no difficulty in finding jurisdiction prior to *Colegrove.* He also analyzed the problem of fashioning an adequate

[20] Emanuel Celler, "Congressional Apportionment—Past, Present, and Future,"
17 *Law and Contemporary Problems* 268 (Spring 1952); Carmine De Sapio,
"The Case for Reapportionment," *Harvard Law Record* 4 (October 24, 1957);
David G. Farrelly and Ivan Hinderaker, "Congressional Reapportionment
and National Power," 17 *Law and Contemporary Problems* 338 (Spring 1952);
Anthony Lewis, "Legislative Apportionment and the Federal Courts," 71
Harvard Law Review 1057 (April 1958); Joey Francis Paschal, "The House
of Representatives: 'Grand Depository of the Democratic Principle'?" 17
Law and Contemporary Problems 276 (Spring 1952); Neil Tabor, "The
Gerrymandering of State and Federal Legislative Districts," 16 *Maryland
Law Review* 277 (Fall 1956); John O. Tilson, "Reapportionment Act of
1929," 31 *Connecticut Bar Journal* 118 (June 1957); James E. Todd, "The
Apportionment Problem Faced by the States," 17 *Law and Contemporary
Problems* 314 (Spring 1952); Walter F. Wilcox, "Last Words on the Ap-
portionment Problem," 17 *Law and Contemporary Problems* 290 (Spring
1952).
[21] Anthony Lewis, "Legislative Apportionment and the Federal Courts," 71
Harvard Law Review 1057 (April 1958).

judicial relief. Courts, he argued, could and should decide apportionment cases. Their injunctive powers were sufficient, he concluded, to impose at-large elections if states failed to respond to declaratory judgments on the unconstitutionality of their respective apportionment plans.

Both scholarly and popular articles also attacked the apportionment problem.[22] Two University of Florida political scientists developed a means of comparing the degree of malapportionment in state legislatures and published a study showing that in every state a minority of voters controlled one or both houses of the legislature.[23] Attention also was focused by other studies on the urban-rural aspects of the problem.[24] Such scholarly studies were underscored by the report of the President's Commission on Intergovernmental Relations in 1955.[25]

Some of the federal courts also were beginning to exhibit reservations about the wisdom of Justice Frankfurter's *Colegrove* opinion. In 1958, a three-judge Minnesota federal court ruled that it possessed jurisdiction to decide an apportionment case. It withheld judgment, however, to allow the state legislature time to act. The legislature acted, and the case became moot.[26] Two years earlier, the federal court for the Territory of Hawaii also asserted jurisdiction.[27] In this case Congress reapportioned the territorial legislature, mooting the case.

Two other significant factors developed during the 1950's. First,

[22] Examples are: George B. Merry, *Christian Science Monitor* (October 2, 6, 9, 13, and 16, 1958; and June 2, 4, 11 and 16, 1959); Richard Lee Strout, "The Next Election is Already Rigged," *Harper's Magazine* (November 1959), p. 35.

[23] Manning J. Dauer and Robert G. Kelsay, "Unrepresentative States," 44 *National Municipal Review* 571 (December 1955).

[24] Gordon E. Baker, *Rural Versus Urban Political Power* (Garden City, N.Y.: Doubleday & Company, Inc., 1955); Bruce Bliven, "The City Boy vs. the Country Boy," *New York Times Magazine*, August 16, 1959; Louis C. Dorweiter, Jr., "Minnesota Farmers Rule Cities," 35 *National Municipal Review* 115 (March 1946). Ralph Eisenberg, "Power of the Rural Vote . . . ," 51 *National Civic Review* 489 (October 1962); Murray C. Havens, *City Versus Farm? Urban-Rural Conflict in the Alabama Legislature* (University, Ala.: Bureau of Public Administration, University of Alabama, 1957).

[25] Commission on Intergovernmental Relations, *A Report to the President* (Washington, D.C.: U.S. Government Printing Office, June 1955).

[26] *McGraw* v. *Donovan*, 159 F. Supp. 901 (D. Minn., 1958); 163 F. Supp. 184 (D. Minn. 1958); 177 F. Supp. 803 (D. Minn. 1958).

[27] *Dyer* v. *Kazuhisa Abe*, 138 F. Supp. 220 (D. Hawaii 1956), reviewed as moot 256 F. 2d 728 (9th Cir. 1958).

the Supreme Court found itself confronted with the desegregation cases. In deciding them, it entered upon an era of expanded use of the Equal Protection Clause of the Fourteenth Amendment. Also, the membership of the Court was transformed between 1953 and 1960. President Eisenhower appointed Earl Warren chief justice, and four new associate justices: William Brennan, Charles Whittaker, John Marshall Harlan, and Potter Stewart. Of the members who sat on the Court when *Colegrove* was decided, only Frankfurter, Black and Douglas remained. Two of the three were dissenters in *Colegrove*.

By 1960, the issue of fair representation was far more prominent than in 1946. But the prospect of action through legislatures was demonstrably hopeless. In state after state, a long list of aborted reapportionment bills could be compiled.[28] But little help seemed forthcoming from the federal courts. If the Supreme Court was to overcome *Colegrove*, the right case at the right time had to be brought.

It also seemed useful to seek action in the state courts rather than the federal courts. First, if the federal courts were asked to rule, they could avoid the question by invoking a doctrine by which a federal court may abstain from deciding a case unless all state remedies have been exhausted. To exhaust all state remedies would require a decision from the state's highest court. Second, many lawyers felt the political question doctrine would be a less formidable problem for state courts than for their federal counterparts.

There was a long history of jurisdiction in the state courts,[29] and it could be argued that the political question doctrine was basically one which dealt only with relations among the branches of the national government. Thus on appeal from a state court, the Supreme Court need not feel the same restraints about congressional power as in the earlier case of congressional redistricting. There was no power in any other branch of the federal government to reapportion a legislature, and since it would have been demonstrated that all state remedies were exhausted, the Supreme Court "must" act.

Based on this strategy, and on the assumption that any case, to be considered favorably, must avoid the danger of being decided too close to an election date, five lawsuits were initiated, independently of each other, in 1959 and 1960.

[28] Scanlan, 38 *Notre Dame Lawyer* 420, 421.
[29] Lewis, 71 *Harvard Law Review* 1057, 1067-68.

In Tennessee, Mayor Ben West of Nashville had been instrumental in bringing suit in state court in 1956. In this case, *Kidd* v. *McCanless,* the state supreme court held that if it acted Tennessee would be left without a valid legislature.[30] The Supreme Court dismissed the appeal.[31] The state court's ruling avoided both the political question doctrine and the federal Equal Protection issue. Tennessee urbanites, however, reinstituted their suit—state remedies now being exhausted—in federal district court. In 1959 a special panel of federal judges split two to one in holding that the federal courts, operating under *Colegrove,* lacked jurisdiction. The dissenting judge argued that *Colegrove* was in error.[32]

August Scholle, the president of the Michigan AFL-CIO, brought suit in his state's courts in 1959. On appeal, a badly split Michigan Supreme Court rejected Scholle's complaint under the *Colegrove* doctrine.[33]

In New Jersey, citizens asked the state courts to order reapportionment of the lower house of the legislature in conformity with the state constitution. The New Jersey Supreme Court, in the summer of 1960, sustained the plaintiffs' position and ordered a reapportionment.[34] While its decision did not reach the federal question, the court said in *dicta* it thought failure to reapportion might well violate the Equal Protection Clause.[35]

In Maryland, Jesse Maury helped found the Maryland Committee for Fair Representation. In August of 1960 the Committee filed a bill of complaint in the state courts; it was dismissed by citing *Colegrove* for lack of jurisdiction.[36] The dismissal was appealed and reached the state's highest court in late 1961.

Peter Straus, the owner of radio station WMCA in New York City, also went to court. He challenged New York's apportionment formula in a case before a three-judge federal court. His suit was dismissed for want of a substantial federal question.[37]

As the cases from Tennessee, Michigan, Maryland, and New

[30] *Kidd* v. *McCanless,* 200 Tenn. 273, 292 S.W. 2d 40 (1956).
[31] *Kidd* v. *McCanless,* 352 U.S. 920 (1956).
[32] *Baker* v. *Carr,* 179 F. Supp. 824 (M.D. Tenn. 1959).
[33] *Scholle* v. *Hare,* 360 Mich. 1, 104 N.W. 2d 63 (1960).
[34] *Asbury Park Press, Inc.* v. *Woolley,* 33 N.J. 1, 161 A. 2d 705 (1960).
[35] 33 N.J. 1, 161 A. 2d 705, 710.
[36] *Maryland Committee for Fair Representation* v. *Tawes,* No. 13, 920 Equity (Circuit Court of Anne Arundel Co., Md., Feb. 21, 1961).
[37] *WMCA* v. *Simon,* 196 F. Supp. 758 (S.D. N.Y. 1961).

York moved toward the Supreme Court, another related case had already arrived. In Tuskegee, Alabama, the Negro population outnumbered the white. Negroes were registering in such numbers that white domination of the city was endangered. To prevent the loss of white power, the Alabama legislature redrew the city boundaries of Tuskegee, excluding all but a few Negroes from the city limits. Negroes brought suit in federal court in the case of *Gomillion* v. *Lightfoot*.[38] The federal court in a 2-1 decision held that, unfortunately for the Negroes, establishing municipal boundaries was a plenary power of the legislature, and the federal courts could do nothing to protect them.[39]

The Supreme Court reversed the federal court. In a unanimous opinion by Mr. Justice Frankfurter, the Court held that the action of the Alabama legislature was proscribed by the Fifteenth Amendment.[40] Frankfurter, keenly aware of the implications that a racial gerrymandering case had for ordinary political gerrymandering and malapportionment, was at great pains to point out the distinctions between *Gomillion* as a Fifteenth Amendment case and the representation issue's Fourteenth Amendment approach.[41] The subtle distinctions were too much for Mr. Justice Whittaker. In a concurring opinion he said the case should have been decided on Equal Protection grounds.[42]

By emphasizing the Fifteenth Amendment in *Gomillion*, Frankfurter avoided a marriage of the concepts of Equal Protection arising from the school desegregation cases and those which were to be raised in the coming reapportionment cases. But in spite of his meticulous hedging of the issues, *Gomillion* was viewed as a gerrymandering case and a case in which the central issues were the effectiveness and equality of the vote and the power of the federal courts to correct a wrong brought about by exercise of a power considered plenary by the legislature.

Gomillion did not really reach the issues in *Colegrove* due to Justice Frankfurter's legal maneuvering. It did weaken *Colegrove*, however. One commentator called *Gomillion* a "Dragon in the

[38] *Gomillion* v. *Lightfoot*, 167 F. Supp. 405 (1958), affirmed 270 F. 2d 594 (1959).
[39] 167 F. Supp. 405, 410.
[40] *Gomillion* v. *Lightfoot*, 364 U.S. 339 (1960).
[41] 364 U.S. 339, 346.
[42] 364 U.S. 339, 349, Mr. Justice Whittaker, concurring.

Thicket." [43] And attorneys for the reapportionment cases' plaintiffs immediately seized upon *Gomillion,* along with the New Jersey case, for support of their arguments in behalf of jurisdiction and the power of the courts to provide relief.

As *Baker* v. *Carr* was readied for petition to the Supreme Court, its initiators sensed the importance of their effort. Here at last was a case with all the elements lacking in *Colegrove.* Tennessee had not reapportioned since 1901. All state remedies were exhausted, including state courts. The next election was more than a year away. The issues were squarely presented, especially the key issue of jurisdiction. It should be remembered that no reapportionment case had yet been considered on its own merits. The only issues really on appeal were whether courts had jurisdiction to decide the issue and whether the problem could be remedied by a court, once it accepted jurisdiction.

When a case is appealed to the Supreme Court it is accompanied by a brief from the losers in the lower court, petitioning the Supreme Court to hear their case. Technically this statement is not supposed to argue the merits of the case. Its purpose is to disclose enough of the case to support the argument that the court has the jurisdiction to hear the case, that a substantial federal question is raised, and that the case is important enough to warrant the time and attention of the Supreme Court. The appellees, who won in the lower court, file a similar statement, answering the appellants, and arguing that the court should not hear the case because it was properly decided in the lower court. On the basis of these statements and the opinions or records of the lower courts, the Supreme Court decides whether it will hear the case or whether it will simply dismiss the petition as had been done in all the apportionment cases since *Colegrove.* If four justices wish to hear the case, it will note "probable jurisdiction," in a published order, and set the case for argument.

The plaintiffs in *Baker* knew they must clear this important first hurdle. They also knew that once the court agreed to hear argument, they must win or the *Colegrove* precedent would almost irretrievably be confirmed. They also knew that the other reapportionment cases depended on their success.

While never conclusive, one important factor in a major con-

[43] Jo Desha Lucas, "Dragon in the Thicket: A Perusal of *Gomillion* v. *Lightfoot,*" in Philip B. Kurland, ed. (Chicago: University of Chicago Press, 1961), p. 194.

stitutional law case is whether it is entered by the Solicitor General of the United States. The Solicitor General is the chief attorney for the United States government. He decides what cases the government will appeal when it loses in the lower courts. His office— not the Attorney General's—reviews all appeals and decides which government attorney will argue them. The Solicitor General himself argues the most important of the government's cases. The office is probably second in importance only to the Supreme Court in the nation's legal system. Because of his great prestige and the extremely high quality of work during the long history of his office, the Solicitor General is received with great respect by the Supreme Court.

One of his important roles is to appear as *amicus curiae* in important cases in which the U.S. is not a party, but in which the Department of Justice determines that the national government has a vital interest. On this basis the Solicitor General entered the school desegregation cases in 1954. His decision to enter as *amicus curiae* lent greater urgency to the case. It increased the likelihood that the Court would hear it. When oral argument is held, the Solicitor General takes part of the time allotted by the Court to argue the point of view of the government. He may support one of the litigants, but his most important function is to advise the Court of the position of the national administration on the issue. The value of his appearance to the Court is in having a separate assessment of the issues. If he takes one side, his value to the favored litigant is immense.

The Tennessee citizens felt their cause would be immeasurably strengthened if the Solicitor General could be persuaded to enter the case as *amicus curiae* in support of their position. They found a receptive Solicitor General in J. Lee Rankin. Rankin felt that *Colegrove* was unwise law. But the Solicitor General's participation in a case involves an administration decision, not just personal interest on his part. Rankin argued for and won a decision to enter the case. In this he was supported by Vice-President Richard Nixon. Nixon's interest was turned toward the case in part by Charles Rhyne, Jr., a distinguished Washington attorney and past president of the American Bar Association. Rhyne was also the president of the National Institute of Municipal Law Officers. In this position he had long been concerned with the reapportionment cause. Because of his position and knowledge of the subject, he was retained as counsel for the plaintiffs in the appeal to the Supreme Court.

His contact with the Vice-President stemmed from a long friendship which began when they were classmates at Duke University Law School.

When Rankin left office with the change of administrations in 1961, his successor, Archibald Cox, sustained his decision and entered the case for the government as *amicus curiae*.

JURISDICTION WITHOUT STANDARDS
Baker v. Carr

So *Baker* reached the Supreme Court and the Solicitor General entered the case as *amicus*. The case dealt with state action (or inaction) alone; all forms of alternative relief had been exhausted; and it built on the expanding doctrine of Equal Protection to construct a case for apportionment based on population. More immediately before the Court than interpretation of the Equal Protection Clause, however, was the problem of defining the proper role of the courts in such issues (if the Frankfurter opinion were to be abandoned). *Baker* also raised the questions of appropriate relief and of the enforceability of court orders.

Baker was argued twice before the Supreme Court. In April of 1961 the Court heard oral argument, but instead of deciding the case, it ordered reargument as the first case of the October 1961 term. Mr. Justice Brennan announced the decision on Monday, March 25, 1962. While the political question doctrine fell, the Court did not explicitly overrule Frankfurter's opinion in *Colegrove*. Speaking for six members of the Court, Brennan decided only the narrow issues: a citizen could sue; federal courts had jurisdiction of the subject matter of apportionment cases; the issue was an appropriate one for courts to decide.

In a lengthy opinion Brennan redefined the political question doctrine. He held that *Colegrove* did not stand for the political question doctrine, but rather by combining the Rutledge opinion with the dissenters, *Colegrove* stood 4 to 3 in favor of jurisdiction and by adding Rutledge to the Frankfurter bloc, it stood 4 to 3 for dismissal on equitable grounds.[44]

Baker established the existence of a federal right to be represented fairly, but it did not define that right. This failure drew

[44] *Baker* v. *Carr*, 369 U.S. 186, 202 (1962).

the fire of two of the majority justices, Tom Clark and William O. Douglas. In separate opinions they argued that the Court should have decided the substantive issues in the case, and both suggested standards for testing the constitutionality of an apportionment plan.[45]

Mr. Justice Stewart, who voted with the majority, also wrote a separate opinion emphasizing the narrowness of the opinion.[46] The two dissenting justices (Mr. Justice Whittaker had become seriously ill and did not participate in the decision), Frankfurter and Harlan, castigated the majority for accepting jurisdiction in the first place, and for failing to clarify the standards for constitutional apportionment once jurisdiction was accepted.[47]

Baker, then, refused to answer the question put by Mr. Justice Douglas: "The extent to which a state may weight one person's vote more heavily than it does another's." [48] It merely said that a person so treated has a right to sue in federal court, and that the court can decide whether his grievance is in fact of such a nature that it violates the Equal Protection Clause. Clearly, lower courts might be required to afford relief if they ruled in favor of the plaintiff. On this problem, Justice Brennan said simply that the courts could fashion appropriate relief within the "well developed and familiar standards" of the Equal Protection Clause.[49]

Mr. Justice Frankfurter's monumental dissent, the last great opinion of his long judicial career, bristled in defense of the political question doctrine he had developed in *Colegrove*. He also caustically assailed the vagaries of the majority decision. The Court, he warned, was involving itself in a nonjudicial role by choosing "among competing bases of representation—ultimately, really, among competitive theories of political philosophy." [50]

The Court, Frankfurter warned in a stream of judicial metaphors, was creating a "mathematical quagmire," and inviting with its absence of standards (which he held could not be devised anyway), a "game of ducks and drakes" between legislatures and courts.[51]

[45] 369 U.S. 186, 241, 251 (1962).
[46] 369 U.S. 186, 265.
[47] 369 U.S. 186, 266.
[48] 369 U.S. 186, 242.
[49] 369 U.S. 186, 226.
[50] 369 U.S. 186, 300.
[51] 369 U.S. 186, 268.

Certainly an element of political philosophy was involved in the choices made by the court in *Baker* v. *Carr*. In performing its political function of interpreting the constitution, the Supreme Court chose one interpretation over another. It would be a mistake, however, to assume that Mr. Justice Frankfurter's position was one of neutrality among philosophical alternatives. In the first instance, his opinion represents one view of the role of the court in American politics. In the second it supports a theory of representation which suggests that there is more value in *flexibility* in establishing apportionment systems than in requiring *equality* of population among representatives' constituencies.

While the decision of the Supreme Court in *Baker* may be seen as a choice of one political theory over that preferred by Mr. Justice Frankfurter in *Colegrove,* it is not just that simple. The issue of political philosophy was itself only partly resolved. Many questions remained, among them those of standards to apply to one or two house legislatures. These standards, moreover, were not to be decided on the basis of pure political philosophy. The issue was now in the courts. Any philosophical requirements must be reconciled with "the well developed and familiar standards" of the Equal Protection Clause. Finally, the conditions which produced the reapportionment impasse did not disappear on the day *Baker* v. *Carr* was handed down. Incumbent legislators looked upon the decision with much less enthusiasm than the plaintiffs or the political science profession. The process of setting and enforcing standards of fair apportionment would not be an automatic one. It would involve a continuing interplay of political theory with constitutional law. And it would be entwined with the hard, real world of politics where the problem was born. The court was in the thicket, and that being so, it was by no means out of the woods.

CONSTITUTIONAL RIGHTS, PRACTICAL POLITICS, AND LEGAL TACTICS

> *The bear went over the mountain . . .*
> *To see what he could see,*
> *But the other side of the mountain . . .*
> *Was all that he could see.*

Old Folk Song

Before *Baker* v. *Carr,* when aggrieved citizens petitioned their legislatures for reapportionment, they were told to go to Hell. Now they did not have to go. *Baker,* more than anything else, broke the inertia of the malapportionment dilemma by making a basic change in the rules of the game. An alternative to legislative relief was now available.

While uncertainties about its specific application remained, *Baker* introduced two new conditions upon that heretofore uncontrollable political environment. A decision now had to be made, and it had to be made within judicially controlled constitutional boundaries. Whatever flexibility remained for legislative discretion had to be found within those bounds. Thus, the major goal of both the advocates and the opponents of reapportionment was to win the battle to decide just how much a limiting factor *Baker* was to be in establishing standards of fair representation. This goal estab lished the bases for competing strategies in politics and in litigation.

The Legal Blitz

In the weeks that followed *Baker,* law suits were begun in many states. Within a year seventy-five cases had been filed in state and federal courts. In many of these cases it is inaccurate to say that the advocates of reapportionment were pursuing a strategy designed to produce a particular result; many cases represented an exuberant

57

release from the hopeless frustration which had been the hallmark of past attempts at apportionment reform. The cumulative effect of the suits was to place the great majority of legislatures under a legal *blitz* emphasizing the necessity of ultimate action. So far as the cases represented a strategy at all it was one of pressing for quick remedial action through the courts themselves or through threat of court action. Most of the plaintiffs had no legislative strategy mapped out to develop specific reapportionment proposals if the courts deferred (as most did) to the legislatures. As a matter of fact, few plaintiffs had very well developed legal strategies.

The initial actions by courts were encouraging. In a number of states court orders upset existing apportionments and ordered into effect or cleared the way for new apportionment plans by the time of the 1962 elections. Following *Baker,* the Maryland Court of Appeals ordered a trial on the merits of the challenge to the existing apportionment,[1] and the lower court declared the House of Delegates unconstitutionally apportioned. But in the absence of specific standards set by the Supreme Court, the trial judge deferred a decision on the apportionment of the senate.[2] Following this decision, a hastily called special session of the General Assembly enacted a stopgap reapportionment to cover the 1962 elections, which gave urban areas nineteen more seats.

In Alabama, a federal district court ruled that the existing apportionment was unconstitutional. After the legislature failed to act satisfactorily, the court ordered into effect for the 1962 elections the most equitable sections of two bills enacted by the legislature as alternative plans.[3]

In Georgia, the state senate's distribution of members was held to be unconstitutional [4] and the legislature reapportioned it. One result of the change was the election of the first Negro state senator since reconstruction days. Also in Georgia, a federal court overturned that state's historic county unit vote system which allowed rural counties to dominate gubernatorial, senatorial, and congressional nominations.[5]

---

[1] *Maryland Committee for Fair Representation* v. *Tawes,* 228 Md. 412, 180 A. 2d 656 (1962).
[2] *Maryland Committee* v. *Tawes,* No. 13, 920 Equity (Circuit Court of Anne Arundel Co., May 24, 1962).
[3] *Sims* v. *Frink,* 208 F. Supp. 431 (M.D. Ala., 1962).
[4] *Toombs* v. *Fortson,* 205 F. Supp. 248 (N.D. Ga. 1962).
[5] *Sanders* v. *Gray,* 203 F. Supp. 158 (N.D. Ga. 1962).

By mid-July, however, the courts became more reluctant to force revisions before the 1962 elections. Docketing problems, appeal problems, and problems of establishing standards were among the reasons the legal blitz faltered.

A few weeks after it decided *Baker* the Supreme Court remanded *Scholle* v. *Hare* to the Michigan Supreme Court.[6] That court held reargument and by a sharply divided five-to-four decision held that both houses of the legislature must be apportioned on the basis of population.[7] Since the Supreme Court of the United States was not in session at the time of the Michigan decision, Justice Stewart who supervised the sixth circuit was petitioned to stay the order until the Supreme Court could hear an appeal.

After hearing argument he ordered that the Michigan decision be stayed.[8] A few days earlier, the Maryland Court of Appeals had held that the Fourteenth Amendment did not require reapportionment of more than one house of the legislature.[9] Courts in Georgia and Florida ruled in the same vein,[10] while courts in Rhode Island,[11] Tennessee,[12] Alabama,[13] and Oklahoma[14] held that the Equal Protection Clause required both houses to be apportioned on a population base.

The major problems of legal strategy left in the wake of *Baker* were rapidly beginning to crystallize. The essential problem was to produce workable and judicially enforceable standards of apportionment under the Equal Protection Clause.[15]

This was essential if the courts were to bear the brunt of the battle. Moreover, there had to be generally agreed upon criteria,

[6] *Scholle* v. *Hare*, 369 U.S. 429 (1962).
[7] *Scholle* v. *Hare*, 367 Mich. 176, 116 N.W. 2d 350 (1962).
[8] *New York Times*, July 28, 1962, p. 9.
[9] *Maryland Committee* v. *Tawes*, 229 Md. 317, 182 A. 2d 877 (1962).
[10] *Toombs* v. *Fortson*, 205 F. Supp. 248 (N.D. Ga. 1962); *Sobel* v. *Adams*, 208 F. Supp. 316 (S.D. Ga. 1962).
[11] *Sweeney* v. *Notte*, 183 A. 2d 296 (R.I. 1962).
[12] *Baker* v. *Carr*, 206 F. Supp. 341 (M.D. Tenn. 1962).
[13] *Sims* v. *Frink*, 208 F. Supp. 431 (M.D. Ala. 1962).
[14] *Moss* v. *Burkhart*, 207 F. Supp. 885 (W.D. Okla. 1962).
[15] For discussion of the problem of devising standards, see Dixon, 27 *Law and Contemporary Problems* 329; Royce Hanson, "Courts in the Thicket: The Problem of Judicial Standards in Apportionment Cases," 12 *American University Law Review* 51 (January 1963); Robert B. McKay, "Political Thickets and Crazy Quilts: Reapportionment and Equal Protection," 61 *Michigan Law Review* 645.

since no two cases could arise in the same court. The pluralism of the court system itself operated to produce varied interpretations of both facts and law.

In the early briefs there had been a general assumption by the plaintiffs that Equal Protection could be equated with the slogan "One Man–One Vote." That feeling had been reinforced by the federal court opinion outlawing Georgia's county unit vote system by which votes for governor and other state officers were weighted through giving an arbitrary number of "unit votes" to each county.[16] But for the courts themselves, and for the scholars writing in the law reviews, the problems implicit in *Baker* could not be resolved for all the states by so simple and sweeping a declaration of the objective of apportionment. While the courts were dealing with a question involving politics, they had to develop their answers within the framework of litigation. They also worked with over forty sets of similar, but distinguishable, data on state representation. The objective of equity is justice rather than complete uniformity of decision, even in the same subject matter area.

As the cases accumulated, and as the same issues emerged cast in different approaches by different courts, the basic problems began to become clear. It was also clear that all the constitutional law issues involved in reapportionment had not been presented to the Supreme Court in *Baker*. The great unanswered question from the Tennessee decision was asked in every courtroom where the issue was tried: what were the standards demanded by the Equal Protection Clause?

Answering this question was a complex matter involving a mixture of analogous reasoning from other Equal Protection cases and perception of facts. Judges pursuing the question normally started from two points: (1) the practical impossibility of achieving mathematical equality in apportionment, and (2) the legal history of the Equal Protection Clause. From these two base points the law must intersect to answer the questions, which in combination would provide the standards to be used in measuring the constitutionality of a state's system of legislative representation. In addition the courts had a series of hints and inferences to follow. The hints were contained in the concurring opinions written by Justices Douglas

[16] *Sanders* v. *Gray*, 203 F. Supp. 158 (N.D. Ga. 1962).

and Clark in *Baker*.[17] The problem was that the hints could lead one in different directions. The inferences could be found in the dissents of Mr. Justice Harlan. His dark broodings about the thinking of the majority in its *per curiam* orders to remand cases to Michigan[18] and New York[19] suggested that the majority of his brethren were enamored of the idea of one man–one vote.

In a given state the essential problem was for a court to decide how much deviation from equality the Fourteenth Amendment permitted as latitude for legislative experimentation or consideration of non-population factors. The answers varied with the state and with the court. An Oklahoma federal court said "substantial equality" was required.[20] The Michigan Supreme Court set the outside limit at two-to-one variations in the extreme.[21] In Delaware, a federal court felt the Fourteenth Amendment as a basic standard required that a majority of the population be able to elect the legislature.[22] And for Delaware, it argued deviations of one and a half to one were the largest allowable.[23]

All the reapportionment cases did not offer gross deviations or widespread disparities. In a few states discrimination was erratic rather than pervasive. In others, the use of formulas which were rational on the surface provided subtle means of assuring one-party control of a legislature or rural domination. In such cases as those presented by New York[24] and Virginia,[25] the kind of evidence the trial court would accept and the way in which it handled *prima facie* cases of discrimination which possibly shifted the burden of proof to the state were major factors in ultimately deciding the case. Technical questions of procedure became entangled with the substantive issue of constitutional apportionment standards.

The second problem which immediately emerged was the question of whether the Equal Protection Clause required apportion-

[17] *Baker* v. *Carr*, 369 U.S. 186, 241, 251 (1962). For a discussion of the hints and inferences, see Hanson, 12 *American University Law Review* 51, and McKay, 61 *Michigan Law Review* 645, 681-700.
[18] *Scholle* v. *Hare*, 369 U.S. 429, 434-35, Mr. Justice Harlan, dissenting.
[19] *WMCA, Inc.* v. *Simon*, 370 U.S. 190 (1962), Mr. Justice Harlan, dissenting.
[20] *Moss* v. *Burkhart*, 207 F. Supp. 885 (W.D. Okla. 1962).
[21] *Scholle* v. *Hare*, 367 Mich. 176, 116 N.W. 2d 350 (1962).
[22] *Sincock* v. *Duffy*, 215 F. Supp. 169 (D. Del. 1962).
[23] 215 F. Supp. 169, 184.
[24] *WMCA, Inc.* v. *Simon*, 208 F. Supp. 368 (S.D. N.Y. 1962).
[25] *Mann* v. *Davis*, 213 F. Supp. 577 (E.D. Va. 1962).

ment of both houses of a bicameral legislature on the basis of population. In his *amicus* brief before the Supreme Court in *Baker* the Solicitor General had written that:

> . . . a state undoubtedly can provide that one chamber of its legislature represents equal areas or governmental subdivisions, even though the result does not approximate equal apportionment.[26]

The question of bicameralism raised in turn that of the analogy between the composition of a state legislature and the federal Congress. As the historical review of representation demonstrated, the analogy was not appropriate. It was, nonetheless, used by the defendants in reapportionment suits as a principal rationalization for malapportionment in one house. The bicameral problem concerned Justice Stewart in his stay of the Michigan decision.[27] Cases in Georgia, Florida, Maryland, Ohio, and Illinois, among others, also foundered on the bicameralism issue.[28]

As the cases developed, however, the preponderance of legal opinion, both from the bench and in the law reviews, held the federal analogy inapplicable and took the position that the Fourteenth Amendment required substantial equality of representation for citizens in both houses of a state legislature.[29]

The Solicitor General (having won his case, as one attorney put it) changed his views on the bicameral question also. In June of 1962, he told the Tennessee Bar Association that if one house were apportioned strictly on a population basis, he thought the courts might ultimately allow some recognition of "historical, political or geographic subdivisions *provided that the departure from equal representation in proportion to population is not too extreme.*" [30]

Still enough doubt remained about the ultimate meaning of Equal Protection for a bicameral legislature to persuade a number

[26] *Brief for the United States as Amicus Curiae, Baker* v. *Carr*, 369 U.S. 186 (1962), pp. 69-70.
[27] *New York Times*, July 28, 1962, p. 9.
[28] *Germano* v. *Kerner*, 220 F. Supp. 230 (N.D. III, E.D. 1962); *Maryland Committee* v. *Tawes*, 229 Md. 406, 184 A. 2d 715 (1962); *Noland* v. *Rhodes* and *Sive* v. *Ellis*, 218 F. Supp. 953 (S.D. Ohio, E.D. 1962); *Sobel* v. *Adams*, 208 F. Supp. 316 (S.D. Fla. 1962); *Toombs* v. *Fortson*, 205 F. Supp. 248 (N.D. Ga. 1962).
[29] See Robert B. McKay, *Reapportionment and the Federal Analogy* (New York: National Municipal League, 1962); McKay, 61 *Michigan Law Review* 645; Hanson, 12 *American University Law Review* 51.
[30] Archibald Cox, "Current Constitutional Issues," 48 *American Bar Association Journal* 711, 712 (1962).

of trial courts and state appellate courts to avoid overturning apportionment of both houses. Where the courts were not persuaded, the bicameral question, being in dispute, provided a convenient basis for an appeal, and, pending the appeal, a stay of the trial court's order to reapportion.

The third basic problem involving Fourteenth Amendment standards regarded cases where the challenged malapportionment resulted, not from the failure to act or the dilatory tactics of the legislature, but from a plan adopted by the people in a referendum, and even initiated by them through a petition. There were two aspects of the problem. In some states, voters had the choice of a plan based on equality of persons and one based on other factors. Should the courts disallow a popular choice as a violation of the right of the individual to equality of political power if the majority clearly had chosen not to keep its power to rule? The second aspect of the problem involved the propriety of court intervention in such cases, where nonjudicial remedies were readily available if a majority of the voters felt they were really inconvenienced by malapportionment. Once again, the courts answered the same question differently, and different answers came even from the same federal judicial circuits.

In Oklahoma, a federal court panel rejected the initiative and referendum arguments. Chief Judge Alfred Murrah of the Tenth Circuit's Court of Appeals declared that ". . . the right asserted here cannot be made to depend upon the will of the majority." [31] But in Colorado, after voters rejected an "equal" plan for an "unequal" Senate apportionment at the 1962 elections, the federal court at Denver stated:

> By majority process the voters have said that minority process in the Senate is what they want. A rejection of their choice is a denial of the will of the majority. If the majority becomes dissatisfied with that which it has created, it can make a change at an election in which each vote counts the same as every other vote.[32]

In both the Oklahoma and Colorado cases issues were raised which justified appeals and consequently either a stay in the court's order or at least uncertainty about the final outcome.

Some judges were extremely sensitive about judicial involvement in the whole reapportionment controversy. Others were simply un-

[31] *Moss* v. *Burkhart*, 207 F. Supp. 885, 894 (W.D. Okla. 1962).
[32] *Lisco* v. *Love*, 219 F. Supp. 922, 926-27 (1963).

prepared to handle reapportionment cases. They expressed their doubts, misgivings, and occasional hostility about judicial handling of the subject matter in their opinions. Judge William L. Henderson, writing for the Maryland Court in the opinion upholding a senate apportionment based on jurisdiction and history, had obvious distaste for the issue and the task of developing Equal Protection standards.[33] In Florida federal Court of Appeals Judge Jones seemed eager to embrace almost any rationale for interfering with legislative judgment.[34] Of the federal courts, those in the South (with the exception of Florida) most fully developed the logic of the Equal Protection Clause in devising standards and tests to measure the constitutionality of legislative apportionments. While a few judges appeared to relish the chance to tackle the problem, most were cautious about fashioning relief, whatever their personal feelings. As a consequence, such judges normally held extensive hearings and used the device of preliminary opinions or observations from the bench to prod the legislature to act. Hearings were occasionally recessed, or final orders not entered until ample time for legislative action had elapsed. While two courts proceeded to decree reapportionment plans, most merely produced guidelines and retained jurisdiction. As the 1962 elections approached, the courts were increasingly reluctant to upset them, and preferred to continue cases until the next year. Certain of ultimate Supreme Court review of this work, judges also were generally reluctant to set precise standards, or to move fast against a lethargic legislature.[35]

The principal value of litigation as a stratagem for attaining reapportionment lay in its promise of ultimate effectiveness, in publicity it provided, and its ability to force a confrontation of the issue. The mounting volume of decisions, and the sometimes forcefully worded opinions combined with legislative fears or uncertainty

[33] *Maryland Committee* v. *Tawes*, 184 A. 2d 715, 720-21.

[34] *Sobel* v. *Adams*, 208 F. Supp. 316, 318. Similar sentiments were expressed by Chief Judge Campbell in *Germano* v. *Kerner*, 220 F. Supp. 230, 234, and by Judge Van Oosterhout in *Davis* v. *Synhorst*, 217 F. Supp. 492, 503, 505 (S.D. Iowa C.D., 1963).

[35] In the Delaware case, for example, the presiding judge held an extensive pre-trial, allowed an intervening special session of the legislature and the 1962 elections to occur without issuing an injunction. The Court then held a one-week trial, compiling a monumental record and extensive evidence, then waited almost four months to issue its opinion, in which it gave the legislature an additional six months to act before entering a final decree. *Sincock* v. *Duffy*, 215 F. Supp. 169 (D. Del., 1963).

about what courts might actually do, were used to spur legislative action where none had been possible before. The basic hope of the legal blitz was to confront the legislature with a compelling deadline and limited alternatives. The basic fault of this stratagem was that those seeking change were frequently unready for the legislative battles which became the usual corollaries of judicial intervention. Practical plans to implement court decrees were not ready. Too much dependence was placed on reluctant courts, and most of the reformers could not match either their legal skill or legal luck with political resources in the legislative arena. They had to be accepted in court as legitimate petitioners. As litigants they were a central part of the judicial process. But the plaintiffs were frequently scorned by the legislatures, which did not consider their intrusion into an "internal" affair appropriate or legitimate. And, unlike the courts, the reformers could not force themselves upon the legislatures.

LEGISLATIVE DELAY, RETREAT, COMPROMISE, AND COUNTERATTACK

The external pressures for change intensified and the constitutional imperatives were now different, even though many issues remained unresolved. *Baker* and its progeny of apportionment cases changed much, but inside the legislatures themselves the basic power structure and the system of internal values remained substantially the same. While some formerly quiescent members were now goaded to demand full compliance with the probable meaning of the Equal Protection Clause, the basic disposition of members still was to do as little as possible. Some members counseled outright defiance of the courts. Others, conceding the inevitability of reapportionment, resolved to eke out as many more elections as possible with as little change as could be had short of open defiance. The strategies of delay and concession followed a variety of courses.

Maryland was the first state to take action after *Baker*. Since the state court would declare only the House of Delegates unconstitutionally apportioned, only that house was changed. The primaries had already been held when the lower court decision was reached. As a result, a stopgap approach of increasing the size of the house was used, rather than a basic redistribution of seats. Nineteen seats were added for the most populous areas. No seats were taken away from the small counties. Although the governor proposed permanent legislation to reapportion the House completely in 1966, this was rejected in the tumultuous special session of the General Assembly.[36] Instead, a final decision was postponed. A special commission was authorized to recommend a solution.[37]

The stopgap legislation was neither fully satisfactory nor constitutional, but it allowed the legislature to buy time. It meant at least one more election without the loss of any of the seats which existed before *Baker*.

Stopgap action to ameliorate the situation for the 1962 elections was only one way of extending the life of the old system. A more common tactic was to enact token adjustments, reallocating a few seats but not making any basic changes in the distribution of legislative power.

One variant of the token adjustment approach was to reapportion rather fully one house, but leave the other unchanged or even increase its malapportionment. This course was taken in Alabama, where the legislature enacted a reapportionment statute making only modest changes in both houses. Fearful of the constitutionality of this act, it then proposed a state constitutional amendment basing the lower house on population, but allocating one senator to each of the sixty-seven counties in the state.

The federal court in Alabama, however, outmaneuvered the legislature in this case. It voided the primary elections which had already been conducted and ordered a new primary held under the provisions of the statute apportioning the senate and the house plan of apportionment in the constitutional amendment.[38] Even this did not provide a full reapportionment, so the legislature acquired some time.

In Virginia, the general assembly had ignored a report of a special commission on apportionment and had made only token adjust-

[36] For a full discussion of the special session, see Royce Hanson, *Fair Representation Comes to Maryland* (New York: McGraw-Hill Book Co., Inc., 1964).

[37] The commission ultimately foundered in disagreement on the means of compliance between the public and legislative members of the commission. Since it had to report in January 1964, a majority of its members urged further postponement of final recommendations until the Supreme Court decided the Maryland case. See *Report of the Commission to Study Reapportionment of the General Assembly* (Annapolis: Office of the Governor, 1964).

[38] *Sims* v. *Frank*, 208 F. Supp. 431.

ments in the representation of the most populous areas of the state in a special session concluded before *Baker*. Although the new apportionment was successfully challenged in federal court, a stay of the decision meant these adjustments were still in effect for the 1963 legislative elections, thereby winning a delay of at least two years in implementation of the court's decision.

In other states, such as New York, the legislature simply refused to act until all legal action was concluded. This sort of inaction bought time enough for at least one more election and often for two. In New York, as in the other states under legal attack, the legislature sought to take advantage of judicial reluctance to reapportion directly the state's representatives. In some ways, such cases seemed to fulfill Justice Frankfurter's prophecy that *Baker* opened the prospect of legislatures' and courts' playing at "ducks and drakes."

While the legislatures proved reluctant, though rarely defiant, in meeting court mandates, an elaborate legal rationale to defend malapportionment was constructed. Heavy reliance was placed on the "federal analogy" as a means of circumventing the thrust of *Baker*. Courts in Georgia,[39] Maryland,[40] Illinois[41] and Ohio[42] upheld malapportionment in one house on the ground that the Constitution could not prohibit a bicameral system of state representation which it required at the federal level. Bicameralism itself depended on using different bases of representation in the separate houses, these courts argued. Dissent in Michigan and Delaware was also based in part on acceptance of the federal analogy.

Other states fabricated new rationales for malapportionment. "Rational" formulas were developed in Michigan and Nebraska allocating eighty per cent of the seats in a house on the basis of population. The remaining twenty per cent were distributed on the basis of area.

Even after a court order had been issued in a case, progress toward reapportionment could be slowed by legitimate disagreements on the details of specific plans. In Wisconsin, a special master appointed by the federal court recommended giving the state more time because honest disagreements between the legislature and the

---

[39] *Toombs* v. *Fortson*, 205 F. Supp. 248.
[40] *Maryland Committee* v. *Tawes*, 229 Md. 406, 184 A. 2d 715.
[41] *Germano* v. *Kerner*, 220 F. Supp. 230.
[42] *Nolan* v. *Rhodes* and *Sive* v. *Ellis*, 318 F. Supp. 953 (S.D. Ohio, E.D. 1963).

governor prevented resolution of the problem.[43] Although the legal
climate had changed radically, the political climate inside the legislature had altered only a few degrees. Urban based proponents of
reapportionment were not always united in interests. Rural strate-
gists found they could occasionally divide pro-reapportionment
votes by favoring one urban area over another, or by establishing a
system of districts which would work to the disadvantage of some
of the incumbent legislators from the urban areas. Reapportionment plans still tended to be worked out on the basis of personal
accommodation. The unwritten rules still were applied as fully as
possible. To be enacted, a reapportionment plan nevertheless required some votes from opponents of any change at all. And for
some legislatures, the partisan or factional advantages of one plan
over others produced bitter disagreements or deadlocks.

For the most part, the governors remained passive spectators,
although the decisions focused new pressures on them. A few, such
as Gaylord Nelson of Wisconsin and J. Howard Edmondson of
Oklahoma, assumed positions of leadership following the Tennessee
decision. Neither succeeded in securing legislation. Edmondson
finally resorted to an initiative petition which was defeated by the
voters. Others, like Buford Ellington of Tennessee, expressed a
curious sort of dual acquiescence—accepting the legitimacy of *Baker*
as law but agreeing to sign whatever plan the legislature might pass.
In Maryland Governor J. Millard Tawes reluctantly demanded the
stopgap action by the legislature, and in Delaware Governor Carvel
helped develop an alteration in the old pattern of apportionment
that fell far short of an acceptable solution. The Delaware plan in
fact increased senate malapportionment while making only modest
improvements in the house. New York's Governor Rockefeller counseled his legislature to postpone any action until all litigation was
complete. And in Virginia, Governor Harrison expressed open hostility to *Baker,* as did a number of other governors.

The governors, long the victims of unrepresentative legislatures,
did not fully use the new weapon the Court had placed at their
disposal. The most plausible reason seemed to be that few governors
were, even after *Baker,* willing to sacrifice other parts of their program in favor of efforts for reapportionment. Once having thought

[43] *Wisconsin* v. *Zimmerman,* 209 F. Supp. 183 (W.D. Wis. 1962); Report of
the Special Master III (August 3, 1962), reproduced in *Court Decisions on
Legislative Apportionment,* II, (New York: National Municipal League,
1962).

reapportionment impossible, most governors now seemed to think it inevitable. In either event, their energies could be more usefully employed elsewhere.

State legislative leaders, meanwhile, realized they could not ultimately win the fight to preserve their power if the courts proceeded to order reapportionment across the country. Soon after *Baker*, a group of state legislators met in Biloxi, Mississippi, at an annual legislative conference sponsored by the Council of State Governments. They decided to launch a massive counterattack against the reapportionment cases and, in part, against the Supreme Court itself.

As ultimately adopted by the legislative assembly of the Council, the legislators proposed three amendments to the federal Constitution. Two of the amendments reflected strong legislative feelings on Supreme Court action issues other than reapportionment; issues such as prayer in public schools and the administration of criminal justice as well as school desegregation. None of the decisions of the Supreme Court in these areas seemed likely to be set aside by constitutional amendment, inasmuch as Congress had to initiate the amendment. So the legislators first urged an amendment to make the constitution easier to amend by permitting two-thirds of the states' legislatures to initiate an amendment, as an alternative to initiation by two-thirds of both houses of Congress.

One proposed amendment struck directly at the Supreme Court. It would have established a "Court of the Union" composed of the chief judges of the fifty highest state courts. This tribunal would be charged with reviewing decisions of the Supreme Court which overruled state constitutions or laws. Lastly, the legislators directly attacked the reapportionment decision by proposing an amendment to withdraw jurisdiction in apportionment cases from the federal courts. Memorials to Congress embodying the amendments were to be introduced on the same day at 1963 State legislative sessions; and their sponsors hoped for quick and dramatic passage. While these actions stirred little comment when they were announced, as legislature after legislature began to memorialize Congress for action on them, pro-court and pro-reapportionment forces became alarmed. Professor Charles Black of the Yale University Law School suggested that they represented an attempt to convert the United States into a confederacy.[44] And Chief Justice

---

[44] Charles L. Black, Jr., "The Proposed Amendment of Article V: A Threatened Disaster," 72 *Yale Law Journal* 957 (April 1963).

Warren lectured the California Bar Association in September of 1963 on the obligations of the bar to the Court.[45]

Ultimately, sixteen states petitioned Congress to enact one or more of the "disunity" amendments. That such extreme action could gain so much support suggests the intensity of legislative feeling in the wake of *Baker*. The amendments failed not just because they were extreme, but because they sought to alter well-accepted constitutional relationships in both the amendment process and the court system. By the summer of 1963, even the sponsors of the amendments considered them impossible to achieve.

THE SECOND ROUND IN COURT:
PHILOSOPHY BECOMES LAW

The jurisdiction conferred by *Baker* brought courts into the thicket but it did not uniformly result in decisions requiring immediate change in every state's apportionment. In a number of states, including Maryland, Ohio, Illinois, New York, Colorado, New Jersey, and Georgia, trial courts or state appellate courts upheld the apportionment of one or both houses of the state legislature. In eight other states, a decision was withheld or postponed, forestalling action and blunting the legal blitz. While partial reapportionment followed court action in some states, litigation had to be continued if there was to be any hope of material change. In a few states, legislatures had responded to court orders. Only in Alabama and Oklahoma had federal judges instituted court devised plans of reapportionment. There were many lawsuits, but few final decisions. Of the first twenty-seven reapportionment cases tried during the year following *Baker,* only seventeen reached a final decision. Of these, only five resulted in clear-cut or complete victory for the challengers.

Once again attention focused on the Supreme Court. By its 1963-1964 term, six apportionment cases and two congressional redistricting cases had reached it. Together the apportionment cases presented the questions left unanswered by *Baker* and answered in conflicting fashion by the trial courts:

1. The reasons for which a state might discriminate in apportionment of representatives;

[45] *New York Times,* Sept. 26, 1963, p. 29.

2. The extent of deviation from equality which might be permitted under the Equal Protection Clause;

3. The applicability of the federal analogy or other rationale to permit use of factors other than population as the sole or primary basis for representation in the second house of a bicameral legislature; and

4. The effect on court intervention of apportionment plans approved through the use of the initiative and referendum.

In addition to these pervasive questions, two other issues were also injected: Should the Court use these cases to decide general guidelines for all cases, or merely decide each case narrowly in its own context without developing a judicial philosophy to guide apportionment? Should the Court require standards more strict than those found to exist at the time of the adoption of the Fourteenth Amendment in 1868?

Now the Supreme Court was to feel from the political system those pressures with which the lower courts had been dealing. In meeting the problem of devising a legal interpretation of the Equal Protection Clause, the Court was also confronted with choices in political philosophy. Those choices, involving the character of representative government, of bicameralism, and of the status of the right of representation in the American Constitution were of great significance. The philosophical choices of the Supreme Court, as the highest constitutional law authority in the Republic, operate as mandates on all officials and private persons subject to its jurisdiction. The Court's value mandates provide the boundaries for political action. The cases before the Court were not just cases at law in which private parties won or lost. They involved basic constitutional issues whose resolution would determine the specific meaning of legislative apportionment in the six states concerned, and the general basis for state legislative representation for the foreseeable future throughout the United States. Political theory was about to become constitutional law, however the Court met the issues.

In November 1963, the Supreme Court heard almost two weeks of oral argument on the reapportionment cases from New York, Alabama, Maryland, Virginia, and Colorado. It also heard argument on the two congressional redistricting cases. The Delaware case was argued a few weeks later. Once again the Solicitor General intervened as *amicus curiae* on behalf of those challenging the old apportionments.

On February 17, 1964, the Frankfurter version of *Colegrove* v. *Green* was finally overturned when the Court decided the Georgia congressional redistricting case, *Wesberry* v. *Sanders*.[46] Although the Court required congressional districts to conform to the one man–one vote concept, it avoided prejudging the state reapportionment cases by basing its decision on Article I of the Constitution instead of the Fourteenth Amendment.[47] The Court also avoided the question of gerrymandering, upholding a New York federal court decision dismissing a complaint of gerrymandering in New York City.[48]

On June 15, 1964, Chief Justice Warren announced the Court's opinions in all six reapportionment cases.[49] The issues had been met squarely by the Court. In the leading case, Alabama's *Reynolds* v. *Sims*, the Court held that "as a basic constitutional standard, the Equal Protection Clause requires that the seats in both houses of a bicameral state legislature must be apportioned on a population basis." The next week, on the basis of *Reynolds*, the Court summarily held nine more legislatures to be unconstitutionally apportioned.[50]

How the Court translated philosophy into law is illustrated by its decisions. It began with the premise that the right of representation was individual and personal in nature. It extracted this premise from earlier judicial recognition that the "right to vote is personal . . ." [51] The right to vote had been protected consistently by the Court. The voting rights cases were cited at length by the Chief Justice.[52] He also reviewed the Court's interpretation of the Fifteenth and Nineteenth Amendments to prohibit a state from debasing the full power of a Negro's or a woman's vote, and its extension of this logic to forbid weighting of votes of citizens in statewide

[46] *Wesberry* v. *Sanders*, 376 U.S. 1 (1964).
[47] 376 U.S. 1, 8.
[48] *Wright* v. *Rockefeller*, 376 U.S. 52.
[49] *Reynolds* v. *Sims*, 377 U.S. 533; *WMCA, Inc.,* v. *Lomenzo*, 377 U.S. 633; *Maryland Committee* v. *Tawes*, 377 U.S. 656; *Davis* v. *Mann*, 377 U.S. 678; *Roman* v. *Sincock*, 377 U.S. 695; *Lucas* v. *Colorado*, 377 U.S. 713 (1964).
[50] *Swann* v. *Adams*, 378 U.S. 553; *Meyers* v. *Thigpen*, 378 U.S. 554; *Nolan* v. *Rhodes*, 378 U.S. 556; *Williams* v. *Moss*, 378 U.S. 558; *Germano* v. *Kerner*, 378 U.S. 560; *Marshall* v. *Hare*, 378 U.S. 561; *Hearne* v. *Smylie*, 378 U.S. 563; *Pinney* v. *Butterworth*, 378 U.S. 564; *Hill* v. *Davis*, 378 U.S. 565 (1964).
[51] *U.S.* v. *Bathgate*, 246 U.S. 220, 227 (1918) as cited in *Reynolds* v. *Sims*, 377 U.S. 533, 561 (1964).
[52] 377 U.S. 533, 554-55.

elections based on place of residence.[53] Finally, he noted that the recent Congressional redistricting case, *Wesberry* v. *Sanders*,[54] "clearly established that the fundamental principle of representative government in this country is one of equal representation for equal numbers of people, without regard to race, sex, economic status, or place of residence within a State." [55] The remaining question was to determine whether the Equal Protection Clause provided "any constitutionally cognizable principles" which could justify departures from the "basic standard of equality among voters" in legislative apportionment.[56]

In reaching a judgment on this question, the Court had some flexibility. Its own precedents in Equal Protection cases tended in two directions. Those cases which dealt primarily with voting rights or other civil rights moved in the direction of tight restrictions against discrimination by increasingly limiting the valid bases on which legislative classifications might be built. In one of the earliest Equal Protection cases, the Court had referred to "the political franchise of voting" as "a fundamental political right, because preservative of all rights." [57] And in *Skinner* v. *Oklahoma,* the Court had refused to uphold an Oklahoma statute which permitted the sterilization of habitual criminals, because the legislative classifications for those subject to the law resulted in dissimilar treatment for crimes essentially the same in character.[58]

The Equal Protection Clause in such cases, as in the school desegregation cases, had been interpreted to prohibit "irrational" or "capricious" classifications which represented deliberate efforts to discriminate against a group of persons or which reflected "no policy." Such cases provided one basis from which Justices Douglas and Clark had constructed their concurring opinions in *Baker,* the latter suggesting judicial standards to prevent "crazy quilt" patterns of apportionment.[59]

A parallel line of cases from which the court could fashion its rule dealt mainly with problems of economic regulation, but overlapped the voting rights area. These cases gave a wide berth for

[53] *Sanders* v. *Gray,* 372 U.S. 368, 379-80 (1963).
[54] 376 U.S. 1.
[55] 377 U.S. 533, 560-61.
[56] 377 U.S. 533, 561.
[57] *Yick Wo* v. *Hopkins,* 118 U.S. 356, 370 (1886).
[58] *Skinner* v. *Oklahoma,* 316 U.S. 535, 536, 541 (1942).
[59] 369 U.S. 186, 241, 251 (1962).

legislative classification, and tended to uphold statutes which asserted or for which could be asserted a reason for classifications resulting in different treatment for individuals affected by the law. A key case in this line of precedents dealt with Sunday closing laws. The basic doctrine of this case, which upheld the laws as an economic or police regulation, was that a classification would be allowed so long as "any state of facts" could be adduced to justify it.[60]

On the borderline between the two groups of precedents was *MacDougall* v. *Green*. This case dealt with political rights, but had been decided in the context of the economic regulation cases in 1948. An Illinois statute required a nominating petition to bear at least two hundred signatures from each of at least fifty counties. Since a petition required twenty-five thousand signatures, this meant that at least forty per cent of all signers would have to be obtained outside one populous jurisdiction such as Cook County (Chicago). In upholding this law the Court declared that the Equal Protection Clause did not prevent a state from requiring "a proper diffusion of political power" among its densely populated and sparsely populated areas.[61]

In the reapportionment cases the Court held tightly to the first line of precedents, even footnoting with approval Mr. Justice Douglas' dissenting opinion in *MacDougall* that a regulation which "discriminates against the residents of the populous counties of the state in favor of the rural sections . . . lacks the equality to which the exercise of political rights is entitled under the Fourteenth Amendment . . . The theme of the Constitution is equality among citizens in the exercise of their political rights." [62]

To meet the standards of the Equal Protection Clause under this line of decisions, certain tests must be passed by any system of legislative classification, such as an apportionment law. First, the law must have as its purpose a permissible objective. Since the Equal Protection Clause required "uniform treatment of persons standing in the same relation to the governmental action questioned or challenged," [63] the constitutionality of any discrimination must grow out of classifications established in order to achieve a permissible objective. What, the Court asked, as had the lower

[60] *McGowan* v. *Maryland*, 366 U.S. 420 (1961).
[61] *MacDougall* v. *Green*, 335 U.S. 281 (1948).
[62] 377 U.S. 533, 564, n. 41, citing 335 U.S. 288, 290 (1948).
[63] 377 U.S. 533, 565.

courts in Alabama, Virginia, and Delaware, is a permissible objective for an apportionment law?

Answering its own question, the Court declared that:

> Since the achieving of fair and effective representation for all citizens is concededly the basic aim of legislative apportionment, we conclude that the Equal Protection Clause guarantees the opportunity for equal participation by all voters in the election of state legislators.[64]

Thus, the Court concluded that discrimination based on place of residence was just as invidious a form of discrimination as that based on race or economic status.[65] "The Equal Protection Clause demands no less than substantially equal state legislative representation for all citizens, of all places as well as of all races." [66]

In choosing to decide that the right of representation was individual and personal, and in refusing to recognize any valid classifications of citizens for the purpose of weighting their legislative representation, the Court essentially predetermined the bicameralism issue. Representation related to the person, not to a county, an area, or an interest. There was no way the Court, starting from the premise of equality, could sanction discriminatory classifications in one house any easier than in the other. The right of equal representation, the Court argued:

> . . . in the election of members of one house of a bicameral state legislature would amount to little if states could effectively submerge the equal-population principle in the apportionment of seats in the other house. If such a scheme were permissible, an individual citizen's ability to exercise an effective voice in the only instrument of state government directly representative of the people might be almost as effectively thwarted as if neither house were apportioned on a population basis.[67]

As for the "federal analogy," the Court simply found it inapposite to state government. It cited the history of state representation, the concept of unitary state government as opposed to federal government at the national level, and the absence of intent by the framers of the Constitution to establish a model for states to follow. "Attempted reliance on the federal analogy," the Court said, "appears often to be little more than a rationalization after the fact

[64] 377 U.S. 533, 565-66.
[65] 377 U.S. 533, 566.
[66] 377 U.S. 533, 568.
[67] 377 U.S. 533, 576.

offered in defense of maladjusted state apportionment arrangements." [68] There could not be, for any suggested reason, a constitutional difference in the bases of representation for the houses of a bicameral legislature.[69]

The Court added, however, that this ruling in no way affected the utility or desirability of bicameralism. Basing both houses on population would not make them identical, it reasoned, and the basic rationale of state bicameralism had not been found in the representation of antithetical interests, but in its use to "insure mature and deliberate consideration of, and to prevent precipitate action on proposed legislative measures." [70]

The Court's reasoning on the basic issue of individual rights also made inevitable its resolution of malapportionment problems resulting from the free choice of the people through the exercise of the initiative and referendum. This was a central issue in the Colorado case: a court of equity might be justified in temporarily postponing judgment or relief to allow use of the initiative or referendum, but the Court held that if a plan of apportionment adopted by referendum fails to satisfy the requirements of the Equal Protection Clause,

> . . . individual constitutional rights cannot be deprived, or denied judicial effectuation, because of the existence of a non-judicial remedy through which relief . . . might be achieved. . . . A citizen's constitutional rights can hardly be infringed simply because a majority of the people choose to do so.[71]

The philosophical position and the basic constitutional rule of the apportionment cases were clear: the right of equal representation was construed to be an individual and personal constitutional right protected by the Equal Protection Clause. This right might not be violated by a state government, either in the name of "balanced" representation through bicameralism or even if a majority of voters preferred to weight the legislative power of some voters greater than others. Having taken this position, the Court was now confronted with the practical problem of devising judicially manageable standards to dispose of the six cases before it and the others waiting decision on its own docket and in the lower courts.

[68] 377 U.S. 533, 573.
[69] 377 U.S. 533, 576.
[70] 377 U.S. 533, 576.
[71] *Lucas* v. *Colorado,* 377 U.S. 713, 736, 737 (1964).

Acknowledging the inefficacy of mathematical exactness as a constitutional standard,[72] the Court also refused to set mathematical limits of permissible deviation from mathematical equality. It declined to ratify the Delaware federal court's standard allowing a range of deviation no greater than one and a half to one. The proper judicial approach, the Court said, was to determine whether in the particular state concerned, "there has been a faithful adherence to a plan of population-based representation, with such minor deviations only as may occur in recognizing certain factors that are free from any taint of arbitrariness or discrimination." [73]

Instead of a formula, the court prescribed some rules of thumb for judicial use. First, it required that a state make "an honest and good faith effort" to apportion both houses on a population basis as nearly "as is practicable." [74] In meeting this basic test of good faith, the court recognized that some variations in population per district would result. It also suggested that in legislative apportionment, it may be more feasible to follow local jurisdictional lines than in congressional redistricting. Such recognition of historic boundaries and local government interests would be constitutional if the resultant apportionment were based "substantially on population and the equal-population principle was not diluted in any significant way." [75] Thus, more flexibility in state reapportionment would probably be allowed by the lower courts than in congressional redistricting. Such matters should not be prejudged, but determined by the lower courts in specific cases. Moreover, the court placed no restriction on the use of multi-member or single-member districts, flotorial districts,[76] or on the use of historic, natural, or political boundaries, so long as deviations from equality connected with their use were based on "legitimate considerations incident to the effectuation of a rational state policy . . . But neither history alone, nor economic or other sorts of group interests, are permissible factors in attempting to justify disparities from population-based representation . . . people, not land or trees or pastures, vote." [77]

The same rule was applied to the question whether it would be

[72] 377 U.S. 533, 577.
[73] *Roman* v. *Sincock,* 377 U.S. 695, 710 (1964).
[74] 377 U.S. 533, 577.
[75] 377 U.S. 533, 578.
[76] In which two or more single districts are joined for the election of an additional representative, often called a "floater."
[77] 377 U.S. 533, 579-80.

constitutional to give separate representation to each of a state's governmental units in at least one house of a legislature. This practice would be a rational and legitimate consideration, but only so long as it was not carried to the extent that "population is submerged as the controlling consideration in the apportionment of seats in the particular legislative body . . ." [78]

Closely related to the use of factors other than population is the matter of formulas which are so complicated or sophisticated that they frustrate analysis on their face. Such a formula was before the court in the New York case, *WMCA* v. *Lomenzo*.[79] In such cases, a court would be required to look at the effect of the use of the formula as well as at the formula itself. Finding that New York's formula resulted in substantial discrimination against urban voters, the Court pointed out that however complicated or sophisticated, an apportionment scheme "cannot . . . result in a significant undervaluation of the votes of certain of a state's citizens merely because of where they happen to reside." [80]

The second basic rule of thumb for measuring constitutionality of an apportionment scheme was developed in the Maryland case. Since the lower court's decision that the house of delegates was unconstitutionally apportioned had not been challenged by the state, the appeal to the Supreme Court dealt basically with the constitutionality of the senate. The state in is arguments had insisted that since the house apportionment was not at issue, it must be assumed to be constitutional. The Court rejected this logic and held that of necessity it must consider the challenged apportionment scheme as a whole. It was not possible, it suggested, to determine the constitutionality of one house's apportionment in the abstract. "Rather, the proper, and indeed indispensable, subject for judicial focus . . . is the overall representation accorded to the State's voters, in both houses of a bicameral state legislature." [81]

In this light, the Court also ruled that whether or not one house was based on population, the Maryland Senate was so grossly unrepresentative that the whole scheme of apportionment was invalid.[82] In an enlightening footnote on this rule contained in the Colorado case, the Court suggested a corollary to its "good faith" rule. A court

[78] 377 U.S. 533, 581.
[79] *WMCA, Inc.* v. *Lomenzo*, 377 U.S. 633 (1964).
[80] 377 U.S. 633, 653.
[81] *Maryland Committee* v. *Tawes*, 377 U.S. 656, 673.
[82] 377 U.S. 656, 673.

must consider the apportionment plan as a whole in deciding if a
"good faith" effort had been made by the legislature to establish
substantially equally populated districts. The Court noted that some
deviations from population in one house might be used to balance
"slight overrepresentation of a particular area in one house with a
minor underrepresentation of that area in the other house." But
even minor, cumulative, instead of offsetting, disparities in both
houses, "may . . . render the apportionment scheme at least constitutionally suspect." [83]

By inference at the very least, the Court decided to judge cases
individually rather than lay down a single, unambiguous, and in-
flexible standard which all states must meet. This approach is
strongly suggested by the fact that the court wrote separate opinions
for each case rather than issuing an opinion in only one case and
deciding the remainder by memorandum orders. Examples were
thus provided for application of the general rules of thumb prescribed. One other issue remained—the relevance of the meaning
to the apportionment controversy of the Fourteenth Amendment at
the time of its adoption.

In the Delaware appeal, the lawyer for the state had introduced
the argument that the construction of the amendment at the time
of its adoption strongly suggested that it was never intended for
use in apportionment cases. Echoing Mr. Justice Frankfurter's dissent in Baker, Delaware contended that there were disparities in
representation in state governments in 1868, and that disparities
existed in the legislatures of southern states "readmitted" to the
Union after they ratified the Fourteenth Amendment. In other
words, Delaware argued that the amendment supported, rather than
forbade, a philosophy of representation which allowed consideration of non-population factors. This argument formed the bulk of
Mr. Justice Harlan's dissent in the reapportionment cases.[84]

In response to this argument, which had also been raised in the
school desegregation cases, the Court held that even if all were not
perfect in 1868, and even though Congress might have implicitly
approved less than fair apportionment plans at the time states were
admitted or readmitted to the Union,

> . . . the Equal Protection Clause can and does require more. . . . Con-
> gress presumably does not assume, in admitting states into the Union,

[83] Lucas, 377 U.S. 713, 735, n. 27.
[84] Reynolds, 377 U.S. 533, 589 (1964).

to pass on all constitutional questions relating to the character of state governmental organization. In any event, Congressional approval, however well-considered, could hardly validate an unconstitutional state legislative apportionment. Congress simply lacks the constitutional power to insulate states from attack with respect to alleged deprivations of individual constitutional rights.[85]

The basic rule that both houses must be apportioned on a population basis seemed unduly harsh or rigid to some critics of the Court's decision.[86] Others felt the Due Process Clause would afford a more flexible standard based on majority rule concepts rather than personal political equality for individual voters which seemed required by Equal Protection.[87] These critics looked at the difficulties for legislatures in meeting the Court's standards. Such difficulties did indeed exist. But the reapportionment decisions, by the nature of the arena in which they were made and by the requirements of translating doctrines of political philosophy into rules of constitutional law, were decisions designed to develop manageable judicial standards rather than convenient legislative equipment.

The Court protected itself and its subordinate courts from endless litigation by developing standards of sufficient clarity discouraging further appeals on the basic distribution of seats. And the standards did seem to be usable for the lower courts in judging the adequacy of both old and new apportionments. Within a year after the reapportionment cases had been decided, seventeen states had completed a reapportionment which was either unchallenged or approved by a court. In twenty-six states existing or newly devised plans had been declared unconstitutional under the standards set in the 1964 cases. Although a number of cases were appealed to the Supreme Court during the 1964-1965 term, the Court heard no further arguments on the basic issues, and normally sustained the lower courts' actions in *per curiam* decisions.

While the question of appropriate relief was not handled explicitly in *Reynolds,* few lower courts actually had to face the pros-

[85] 377 U.S. 533, 582.
[86] For the most effective statements of this position, see Robert G. Dixon, Jr., "Reapportionment in the Supreme Court and Congress: Constitutional Struggle for Fair Representation," 63 *Michigan Law Review* 209 (1964); Cornelius B. Kennedy, "Reapportionment Decisions: A Constitutional Amendment is Needed," 51 *American Bar Association Journal* 128 (February 1965).
[87] Dixon, 63 *Michigan Law Review* 209; and Dixon, "Reapportionment Perspectives: What is Fair Representation?" 51 *American Bar Association Journal* 319 (April, 1965).

pect of constructing a reapportionment plan themselves. Normally an injunction against elections based on the old systems or the imposition of a deadline for action was sufficient to produce action from an unhappy legislature. Some of the relief granted or proposed by judges revealed both a sense of imagination and a sense of humor. In Connecticut, the court appointed as a special master the director of the state university computer center. He was directed to reapportion the state by computer if the legislature failed to act. It acted. In Virginia and New York, courts ordered special elections to speed completion of reapportionment. And in Oklahoma, the court appointed a former president of the League of Women Voters (derisively called "a housewife" by a condemnatory resolution in the state senate) as an advisor in drawing up a court imposed reapportionment plan which it put into effect for the 1964 elections. The speaker of the Oklahoma House of Representatives later told the Texas legislature to "do something" themselves, because, he said, no matter how bad reapportionment might seem, it would be even worse if the court did it.

The courts were speaking. Their messages were increasingly clear: Reapportion, or else!

THE POLITICS AND
SEMANTICS OF CONSTITUTIONALISM

The more you explain it, the more I don't understand it.

Mark Twain

Within hours after the Chief Justice announced the reapportionment decisions, the reaction began. In the week between *Reynolds* and the *per curiam* orders on nine additional cases, members of Congress had demanded a constitutional amendment to allow one house of a legislature to depart from a population basis, the lieutenant governor of Texas had called on his counterparts in other states to seek congressional relief from the ruling on state senates, and Senator Everett Dirksen had ordered his staff to study the feasibility of amending the constitution to nullify the Court's action.

In the remaining days of June and during July, resentment of the decision increased. Dirksen and House minority leader Charles Halleck pledged to lead a fight to overturn or limit *Reynolds* and *Lucas,* and Congressman William McCullough, the ranking Republican member of the House Committee on the Judiciary introduced a constitutional amendment allowing one house to be based on a basis other than population if such a plan were approved by a referendum.[1] The Midwestern Conference of the Council of State Governments blasted the apportionment ruling and urged an amendment guaranteeing the states the exclusive right to determine how their legislatures should be apportioned.

And at the Republican National Convention in San Francisco, Dirksen was joined by Governors Romney (Michigan) and Scranton (Pennsylvania) in urging an amendment. No opposition to their position was stated and the convention adopted a platform plank urging a McCullough-type amendment and proposing a legislative

[1] H.J. Res. 1055, 88th Congress, 2d Session (June 24, 1964).

82

moratorium on federal court action until such an amendment might be ratified.

CHANGING THE ARENA:
THE THICKET GOES TO CONGRESS

Following the Republican Convention, the battle over reapportionment shifted from legislatures and courts to the Congress. Court action of course continued in the majority of the states, but in most cases court action was completed by late summer or the courts' reapportionment orders were stayed until after completion of the 1965 legislative sessions.

The basic problem for the opponents of the Court decisions was timing. While there was general agreement among them on the need to limit or nullify the decisions, Congress was near the end of its session in an election year. It faced a recess in August for the Democratic national convention. Yet, if anti-court action were to succeed, its adherents felt it necessary to place an amendment before the legislatures for ratification before they were reapportioned. A constitutional amendment generally required several weeks of hearings in each house, however, plus a great deal of work on its specific language to assure its obtaining the two-thirds vote of both houses needed for initiation and to allow reasonable confidence that the amendment would accomplish its purposes if ratified by the states.

Although the House Judiciary Committee held a few days of hearings on the McCullough Amendment in late July, Chairman Emanuel Celler opposed the amendment and progress in the House seemed unlikely. Senator Dirksen introduced a Senate companion for the McCullough Amendment,[2] and Congressman William Tuck (D. Va.) introduced a House bill to strip the federal courts of jurisdiction in apportionment cases.[3] None of these approaches seemed likely to succeed in the time remaining before Congress adjourned. If nothing occurred to prevent it, federal and state courts would proceed to reapportion legislatures and the chances for an amendment would be reduced with each reapportionment.

On August 3, Dirksen produced a new formula to prevent court

[2] S.J. Res. 185, 88th Congress, 2d Session (July 23, 1964).
[3] H.R. 11625, 88th Congress, 2d Session (June 16, 1964).

ordered reapportionment. He introduced a bill which provided that in any state where the apportionment of either legislative house was under court attack, any decision by a court would be stayed until the end of the second regular session of the legislature following the enactment of his bill.[4] For all states, this would have placed a two-year moratorium on reapportionment, and in most states, where regular sessions are held only biennially, it would have allowed a four year delay in the enforcement of court ordered reapportionment. Senator Dirksen cheerfully explained that his bill was designed to "prevent chaos" in the states resulting from "precipitate" action by the courts, and its main purpose was to allow a "breathing spell" during which time a constitutional amendment might be considered.[5]

In a surprise move the next day the Republican leader obtained approval of his bill by the Senate Judiciary Committee by a vote of 10 to 2. Only Senators Philip Hart (D., Mich.) and Quinton Burdick (D., N.D.) voted against reporting the bill on which no hearings had been held.[6] Dirksen then announced he would offer his bill as an amendment—or "rider" since it was not germane—to the administration's foreign aid authorization bill.

This was an adroit move on Dirksen's part. The foreign aid bill was "must" legislation for the administration. It had been skillfully steered through the House, where hostility to the program was traditionally greater than in the Senate. Non-germane amendments are forbidden by House rules but permitted in the Senate.

Given the nearness of the end of Congress, a conference would be required on the foreign aid bill. The conference would almost be forced to accept the Dirksen rider as the price of Senate concurrence in the authorization. Moreover, with the end of Congress so imminent and an election campaign already begun, the President would hardly be in a position to veto his foreign aid bill in order to kill the Dirksen rider. There would be neither the votes to override the veto nor time to move a new bill through Congress before adjournment. Also, placing the rider on the foreign aid bill made the position of the liberal Democrats painful and forced a decision whether to vote against a program they advocated in order to prevent a moratorium on reapportionment.

Pro-reapportionment forces immediately denounced Dirksen's

[4] S.R. 3069, 88th Congress, 2d Session (June 16, 1964).
[5] 88th Congress, 2d Session, 110 *Congressional Record,* 17189-91 (1964).
[6] S.R. 1328, 88th Congress, 2d Session (1964).

rider. Representative Celler thought it probably was unconstitutional. The Democratic Study Group in the House of Representatives obtained signatures of over sixty liberal Democrats to a statement saying they would vote against the foreign aid authorization if the Dirksen rider were attached to it. While Speaker McCormack announced his opposition, Carl Albert, the House Majority Leader, along with the Republican leadership, supported Dirksen. And in the Senate, Majority Leader Mike Mansfield indicated his support of some type of moratorium on the courts. A small group of Senate liberals including Senators Hart, Douglas, Clark, Proxmire, and Nelson threatened to filibuster to prevent adoption of the rider and a group of law school deans wired Dirksen and Mansfield their objections to the rider as an attempt to set aside a constitutional decision without an amendment.

The administration was now concerned about the foreign aid bill and Mansfield and Dirksen conferred with Deputy Attorney General Katzenbach and Solicitor General Cox to attempt to develop a compromise which the administration could accept. After three days of negotiations, a compromise was engineered which would allow a stay of court proceedings to permit holding of the 1964 elections on the basis of existing apportionments. The compromise also allowed the legislatures a "reasonable" opportunity in regular session to reapportion, and it allowed the people of a state a reasonable amount of time to comply with any court order through adoption of a state constitutional amendment. Mansfield co-sponsored the compromise with Dirksen.

In the meantime, the House Rules Committee chairman, Howard W. Smith, invoked a little used House rule and on August 13 the Rules Committee, over the strenuous objection of Chairman Celler, relieved the Judiciary Committee of its possession of the Tuck bill which withdrew federal court jurisdiction over reapportionment.[7] By a 10 to 4 vote, the Rules Committee sent the Tuck bill to the House floor.

The Tuck bill was far more sweeping in its effect than the Dirksen rider. It represented a frontal legislative assault on the federal judiciary, and particularly on the Supreme Court. Only once in its history had the Congress enacted legislation withdrawing appellate jurisdiction from the Supreme Court. That action occurred during the reconstruction period when Congress withdrew the jurisdiction

[7] H.R. 1799, 88th Congress, 2d Session (1964).

of the Supreme Court to hear appeals from the federal circuit courts dealing with the reconstruction acts.[8]

While the Constitution gives Congress the power to determine the appellate jurisdiction of the Supreme Court, there remains unresolved the question whether Congress can deprive the Supreme Court, or the federal courts, of jurisdiction of cases "arising under this constitution," particularly where basic constitutional rights are involved. The opponents of the Tuck bill thus argued that it was of dubious constitutionality, while its proponents maintained it was necessary to prevent judicial usurpation of legislative functions and that it was clearly within the purview of Congress so to limit the Court. Nevertheless, some members who were opposed to the reapportionment decisions were unwilling to bridle the courts in so blunt a fashion as Tuck proposed.

When the bill came before the House on August 19, attempts were made to substitute a Dirksen-like moratorium for the stern Tuck approach. But all such efforts were rebuffed since the strategy of opponents of the Tuck bill was to allow it to remain in as strong a form as possible to encumber its chances of passage in either house. The only amendment adopted was one halting all pending reapportionment cases.

After extensive debate, the Tuck bill was passed in the House by a vote of 218 to 175. Ninety-one Democrats joined 127 Republicans to vote for the measure while 140 Democrats and thirty-five Republicans opposed it.[9]

In the Senate, the attacks on the Dirksen rider continued. No enthusiasm could be found for the Tuck bill, although Senator Strom Thurmond sought to bring it before the Senate. The tactic of pro-reapportionment forces was to speak briefly each day on the Dirksen rider and to prepare for a full scale filibuster if necessary. This action eventually forced Mansfield to abandon his plans for adjournment of Congress before the Democratic convention and to set aside the foreign aid bill until after the convention.

Pro-reapportionment forces were also bringing pressure to bear on the administration. The president of the U.S. Conference of

[8] H. Res. 845, 110 Congressional Record, 18772. For a discussion of this action and the conditions surrounding it, see Alfred H. Kelly and Winifred A. Harbison, The American Constitution (New York: W. W. Norton & Co. Inc., 1955), pp. 479-480; also see Exparte McCardle 7 Wall. 506 (1869).

[9] 110 Congressional Record 19666-67 (1964). The record of the debate begins on p. 19580.

Mayors called on Attorney General Robert Kennedy for his support. Other urban based leaders urged the President to oppose the rider. The opposing senators refused to drop their fight against the rider, and attention now began to focus on the Democratic platform hearings.

Although Carl Albert, the House Majority Leader, was chairman of the platform committee, Senators Hart and Clark appeared capable of mustering a majority of the drafting committee and of the full committee for a strong plank in support of the one-man one-vote rule and opposing any constitutional amendment. It was clear that this or any other plank on the reapportionment question would almost certainly insure a bitter floor fight at the convention.

Since the President's agents wished to avoid a platform fight, an understanding was reached with the pro-reapportionment forces on the platform committee. In return for a silent platform on reapportionment, administration assistance would be available to defeat the Dirksen rider.

After Congress reconvened following the convention, Dirksen filed a cloture petition to shut off debate on the rider.[10] At this point, President Johnson let it be known he preferred that the Senate adopt a "sense of Congress" resolution as a compromise. Such a resolution would have no legal effect on the courts, but would allow an expression of congressional opinion on the subject.

Senator Hubert H. Humphrey, the Democratic vice-presidential nominee, co-sponsored such a resolution with Senators Jacob Javits R., N.Y.) and Eugene McCarthy (D., Minn.) as a substitute for the Dirksen rider.[11] Their substitute declared it to be the "sense of Congress" that courts should allow the states adequate time in which to conform to the *Reynolds* decision, and that the states be given time to consider any proposed amendment on legislative apportionment.

On September 10, the Senate refused, by a vote of 63-30, to invoke cloture on the Dirksen rider.[12] With Dirksen's approval, Senator George Aiken (R., Vt.) then moved to table the rider. This move was made in order to show, through the vote against tabling, that a majority of the Senate favored the rider. Aiken's motion

[10] 110 *Congressional Record* 21025-40, 21040-57 (Sept. 8, 1964).
[11] 110 *Congressional Record* 21095 (Sept. 9, 1964).
[12] 110 *Congressional Record* 21236 (Sept. 10, 1964).

failed by a vote of 49-38, falling short of Dirksen's expectations of support.[13] McCarthy then offered the substitute.[14]

Negotiations over the substitute occupied several days. The filibusters objected to any provision which would suspend, or even urge suspension, of judicial decrees while the legislatures considered a constitutional amendment. Finally, agreement was reached to substitute a "sense of Congress" resolution for the Dirksen rider which would suggest that the courts allow legislatures "reasonable time" to comply with their orders, and that "in the event" an amendment was submitted, the courts take this fact into consideration. The Senate, however, rejected this substitute 42-40[15] and also rejected by a vote of 56-21 Senator Thurmond's attempt to substitute the Tuck bill for the Dirksen rider.[16]

While the Rules Committee of the House again discharged the Judiciary Committee of an anti-reapportionment constitutional amendment,[17] Senators Dirksen and Mansfield went to work on another substitute rider. This time they directed the courts in the absence of unusual circumstances to allow legislatures a reasonable time to comply with orders (a legislative session plus thirty days). The new proposal would not disturb any court order issued before September 20 and would permit states where no orders were entered to conduct the 1964 elections under existing apportionment laws. As a sweetener for its opponents, the new version of the rider provided that if the legislatures did not act in the time allowed, the courts themselves would be required to reapportion.

Liberals still objected to the rider, but Senator Mansfield introduced it and obtained agreement to have the Senate vote on it. Dirksen was now unhappy, however, because a sense of Congress resolution lacked the force of law. By a vote of 44-38, the Senate approved the Mansfield resolution on September 24.[18] The foreign aid bill was now passed and sent to Conference where the entire rider was stricken in the Conference report. Congress adjourned without further action on reapportionment.

Several things became clear, however, from the Dirksen rider and Tuck Bill debates. First there was considerable and intense

[13] 110 *Congressional Record* 21241.
[14] 110 *Congressional Record* 21308.
[15] 110 *Congressional Record* 21421 (Sept. 15, 1964).
[16] 110 *Congressional Record* 21430.
[17] H. Res. 848, 110 *Congressional Record* 21667-78 (1964).
[18] 110 *Congressional Record* 22051 (1964).

feeling in both houses for some modification of the reapportionment decisions. If this feeling were to be translated into action,
great care would be required in developing the proper language.

The foes of reapportionment were not united. With the defeat of
the Dirksen and Tuck efforts, there developed agreement that a
constitutional amendment was the only practicable approach to
limiting the court decisions. Ironically, there seemed to be more
support for the idea of an amendment than for the stopgap approaches tried in the late days of the 88th Congress. But to obtain
the two-thirds support necessary for passage, an amendment had to
be very carefully worded. Finally, there seemed to be general agreement that an amendment would have to be initiated by Congress
not later than 1965 if it was to save many legislatures from reapportionment of both houses.

As to the amendment itself, there now seemed general acceptance
in Congress that *Baker,* which acknowledged jurisdiction over apportionment, should be left basically intact. Many Congressmen
felt, however, that *Reynolds* did not leave the states enough latitude in apportioning their senates. The one-man one-vote rule for
one house of a legislature excited little real opposition. The *Lucas*
rule seemed to elicit the greatest opposition in Congress because it
allowed a court to upset an apportionment approved by a referendum.

A STRATEGY FOR REACTION

Powerful opposition to *Reynolds* continued to build during late
1964. The American Farm Bureau Federation and the Chamber of
Commerce of the United States endorsed a constitutional amendment limiting the effect of *Reynolds.* A group of lieutenant governors and the Southern Governor's Conference endorsed the amendment idea. And the national legislative conference of the Council
of State Governments (the same group that sponsored the three
1963 amendments) advocated an amendment. At the urging of state
legislators, the Council of State Governments made the constitutional amendment part of their 1965 legislative program.[19]

[19] *New York Times,* Dec. 6, 1964, p. 66. In January, 1964, a group of state
legislators formed an organization to oppose the expected ruling in the
reapportionment cases. The National Commission on Constitutional Government was organized by forty-nine legislators from various states in a meet-

At the December 1964 meeting of the Council of State Governments in Chicago, a new strategy was developed. The basic objective was a constitutional amendment. No attempt would be made to end court jurisdiction, and apportionment of one house on a population base would be conceded. The imperative was to prevent reapportionment of the second house.

The new strategy was highly realistic. The basic attack would be against the rule in *Lucas,* which set aside a referendum-approved apportionment scheme. The favored amendment then would allow factors other than population for apportionment of one house if approved by voters in a referendum.

The strategy was not one of frontal assault, but a flanking action. A plausible argument could be made that the Court had "gone too far" in adopting one-man one-vote as the standard applicable to both houses. The federal analogy myth provided convenient support for such a theory. Moreover, the attractiveness of an amendment could be enhanced by the provision for referendum approval of a non-population plan. This allowed the sponsors of the amendment to be simultaneously champions of minority rights (by using "other factors") and of majority rule (by advocating a referendum). The sovereign people of the states, the argument was to run, should be allowed to choose the type of representative system they preferred.

The second aspect of strategy was even more ingenious than the content of the proposed amendment itself. The federal Constitution provides for its own amendment through initiation by two-thirds of both houses of Congress, followed by ratification by three-fourths of the states, either through their legislatures or through ratification conventions. All amendments have been added by these methods. But a second method for amendment is also provided by Article V. If two-thirds of the states apply to Congress to call a national constitutional convention, the constitution requires that "Congress shall call a convention for the purpose of proposing amendments. . . ." The Council of State Governments therefore proposed that the state legislatures send to Congress identical applications for a convention for the purpose of submitting the anti-reapportionment amendment to the states for ratification.

---

ing at Lincoln, Nebraska. Hal Bridenbaugh, a Nebraska state senator, was named president and Thomas Graham, Speaker of the Missouri House of Representatives, became executive director. See Peter Irons, "The Race to Control the States," *The Progressive* (May 17, 1965), pp. 11-14.

The objective of this maneuver was not, of course, a national constitutional convention. Such an assembly could probably not be limited by its call. It might consider any amendments or even rewrite the entire constitution. Since this procedure had never been used in amending the constitution, no one seemed quite sure how it would work, whether Congress would respond, the form the "applications" should take, or how the convention, if called, would be apportioned and organized. Congress alone could decide these questions.

The purpose of the identical applications, however, was not to obtain the convention, but to use the application device as a threat to speed action in the regular amending process. Congress was to be faced with the choice of acting to amend on its own initiative, or being faced with a constitutional mandate to open a pandora's box by calling a convention. Four legislatures which were in session in December readily approved applications. The stage was set for the last act of the constitutional struggle over reapportionment of state legislatures.

COUNTER STRATEGY

In late December, Senator Paul Douglas (D., Ill.) took the initiative in calling together a small group of pro-reapportionment leaders including representatives of industrial unions, the American Civil Liberties Union, Americans for Democratic Action, the Conference of Mayors, senatorial offices, and the Maryland reapportionment movement. Initially, the group established a correspondence network among the states to keep Douglas, Hart, and others informed on the progress of the constitutional convention applications. The group decided to act as a leadership group, coordinating the activities of labor, political, civic, and religious groups in opposing a constitutional amendment, rather than to organize formally as a mass membership group.

An early assessment of senatorial attitudes indicated that an amendment such as the Council of State Governments proposed had an exceedingly good chance of passing the Senate and that there was at least a possibility of House passage. The pressure for constitutional amendment came largely from states which had not yet reapportioned. If action on an amendment could be delayed, the pressure seemed likely to subside as more legislatures were reapportioned. The basic stratagem for the pro-reapportionment interests had to be delay. Secondly, Congressmen, especially Senators, had to be shown that major groups were deeply interested in the preservation of the one-man one-vote rule.

The new group, calling itself the National Committee for Fair Representation, alerted friends of reapportionment in the states about the convention resolutions, urged their local organizations to contact members of Congress on the subject, and published a pamphlet attacking the proposed amendment. It also began to mobilize the support of national organizations interested in civil rights.

THE DIRKSEN AMENDMENT

When Congress convened in January, Senator Dirksen introduced his version of the amendment. Senate Joint Resolution 2 carried the names of all thirty-two Republican Senators except Jacob Javits (N.Y.) and Clifford Case (N.J.). Javits introduced his own version.[20] Within two weeks, the Dirksen amendment had collected forty-two co-sponsors.

The new Dirksen amendment had three basic features. The first sentence declared that "the right and power to determine the composition of the legislature of a State and the apportionment of the membership thereof shall remain in the people of that State." By implication, at least, this sentence seemed to eliminate judicial review over the apportionment of either legislative house.

Secondly, the Dirksen amendment asserted that "Nothing in this Constitution shall prohibit" a state from using "factors other than population" in apportioning one house of a bicameral legislature or from giving "reasonable weight" to non-population factors in a unicameral legislature. While these "other factors" were not defined, their acceptability was made contingent upon the third element of the amendment: any "other factors" plan must be approved by the people of the state in a referendum.

The Dirksen amendment was referred to the Constitutional Amendments Subcommittee of the Senate Judiciary Committee, chaired by Senator Birch Bayh (D., Ind.). Its membership included

---

[20] S.J. Res. 44, 89th Congress, 1st Session (1964). Senator Frank Church (D. Idaho) also introduced two versions of an amendment, S.J. Res. 37 and S.J. Res. 38.

a battery of the amendment's co-sponsors and likely supporters. In addition to the three Republicans—Dirksen, Roman Hruska, and Hiram Fong—Democrats James O. Eastland, Sam Ervin, and a later addition, George Smathers, were certain supporters for the amendment. The only sure vote in opposition was freshman Democratic Senator Joseph D. Tydings (Md.). Bayh and Thomas Dodd (Conn.) were not committed at that point.

Fortunately for the supporters of reapportionment, the Bayh subcommittee's first month was occupied with work on the presidential disability amendment. The National Committee for Fair Representation decided, after exploring the issue at some length, to urge hearings on the amendment, and to attempt to persuade Bayh to extend them as long as possible. Their cause was aided by the prolonged Senate action on the 1965 voting rights bill, which occupied the time of many committee members, particularly Dirksen. As a result of these circumstances, Bayh was unable to start hearings on the Dirksen amendment until March.

In the meantime, support for the amendment reached a peak. Spurred by the National Commission on Constitutional Government, a lobbying delegation from the California legislature was sent on a tour of state capitals. State farm bureaus and business organizations also pushed the convention resolution with much success among the disgruntled legislatures. State after state sent "applications" for a convention to Congress. By the time Bayh started hearings, more than twenty legislatures had demanded a convention.

In early February, the American Bar Association endorsed the Dirksen Amendment in a close vote (115-94). The ABA vote was engineered by its past president, John C. Satterfield, a bitter opponent of the Supreme Court's recent decisions and of legislation on civil rights. And shortly after hearings started, the generally liberally oriented National Farmers' Union overruled its leaders and backed the Dirksen amendment.[21]

The first days of hearings were dominated by congressmen who favored the amendment and delegations from state legislatures urging its passage. It was becoming clear to reapportionment leaders that the amendment would be approved unless stronger action was taken. Organized labor had to give the issue highest priority, and church and civil rights groups had to be made aware of the significance of the amendment for Negro and other minority rights

[21] *New York Times*, March 18, 1965, p. 19.

and for state legislative programs in which they were interested. The task was both educational and political.

The Dirksen amendment wove together some potent political values. These were repeatedly stressed in the testimony and in Senator Hruska's meticulous examination of witnesses hostile to the amendment. The hearings thus became a forum for the manipulation of symbols and values relevant to the American political system. The contestants used their respective value positions to enhance their support or opposition to the amendment and to attract other backers.

The basic argument of the sponsors of the amendment was that the people should decide what kind of representative system they wanted. All the amendment did, Senator Dirksen maintained in his testimony before the committee, was to "simply provide states with an alternative by reserving to the people of each state the right to apportion one house of their state legislature on factors other than population if a majority of the people . . . elected to do so." [22]

Dirksen emphasized that his resolution was not intended to overturn the reapportionment decisions. In questioning witnesses, Hruska repeatedly stressed that the amendment recognized and protected popular sovereignty, and allowed the people to choose by the method of one-man one-vote the kind of government they wanted. Hruska also stressed his "confidence" in the people to make the proper decision.

Tactically this position sought to place opponents of the amendment at a disadvantage—to make them appear fearful of the people and enemies of the doctrine of popular sovereignty. The opponents of the amendment could assert competing values, however, to counter the basic thrust of the Dirksen-Hruska approach. They argued that the right to representation was a fundamental right, and like such basic rights as free speech, it should not be abridged, either by legislatures or by the people through referendum. By allowing a referendum on apportionment, they argued that the Dirksen amendment did indeed nullify or limit the Supreme Court's decision—particularly its ability to protect any person against majority abuse. The first sentence of the amendment was repeatedly assailed as an attempt to remove all jurisdiction from the courts.

[22] Testimony of Senator Dirksen in *Reapportionment of State Legislatures,* Hearings before the Senate Subcommittee on Constitutional Amendments, 89th Congress, 1st Session (1965), p. 8.

While this intent was repeatedly denied, Senator Hruska eventually stated his opinion that the sentence should be withdrawn.

Both sides also championed the value of preserving the rights of minorities against majority domination. Supporters of the amendment conjured all manner of situations in which remote and sparsely populated areas would be virtually unrepresented although their area and its economy were essential to the state. People in such areas would find their representative unaccessible because of the great size of their legislative district. They might also find their interests submerged by being combined with others in great heterogeneous districts almost impossible to represent. The urban majority would just ignore minority interests if the Supreme Court decision stood.

While refuting these arguments by pointing to the latitude left for "other factors" in the *Reynolds* decision and pointing out that the difficulties of representing a heterogeneous rural area are not much greater than representing a complex urban area, the amendment's opponents championed minority rights also. Aside from arguing that representation was an individual right, they argued that the language "nothing in this constitution," combined with the ambiguity of the phrase "factors other than population," could make possible apportionments discriminating against Negro voters or other minorities in order to reduce their influence in state politics. They raised the question whether such broad language would overrule the Fourteenth and Fifteenth Amendments' restrictions on discrimination, as well as prevent judicial review of any apportionment plan adopted under the proposed amendment. Even if overtly racial schemes were outlawed, the use of "other factors" such as education, wealth, or property ownership could be used with the effect of severely diluting newly won Negro voting strength.

The National Committee for Fair Representation witnesses stressed this point, and the committee's leaders worked to produce other witnesses to testify to its philosophical, constitutional, and civil rights objections to the amendments. With the continued efforts of Senator Tydings, the hearings were extended to hear more witnesses opposing the amendment. Among those that the National Committee and Tydings secured were former Solicitor General Rankin, Burke Marshall (former assistant Attorney General for Civil Rights), and Clarence Mitchell, the Washington representative of the NAACP. Meanwhile, the National Council of Churches denounced the Dirksen amendment and labor and civil rights groups intensified their lobbying against it in spite of their understandable preoccupation with the still pending voting rights legislation.

Senator Tydings also resolved to take more dramatic action since the poorly attended hearings had stirred little notice. He decided to deliver his maiden speech on the floor of the Senate on the Dirksen Amendment soon after the Senate passed the voting rights bill. He gave a long, scholarly address emphasizing the disparity between the amendment and the action just taken by the Senate on voting rights. The reprinted speech also became a valuable piece of material for the Fair Representation Committee and other groups fighting the Dirksen Amendment. Tydings' speech catalogued the objections to the bill before the subcommittee:

1. The first sentence eliminated judicial review.

2. The vagueness of "other factors" would allow discrimination against Negroes and other minorities.

3. The right of representation should not be submitted to a referendum.

4. Even if it should be submitted, the Dirksen Amendment made no provision for subsequent review by the people, thus freezing a malapportionment for all time.

5. Such an amendment should not be referred to the legislatures with a vested interest in continuing malapportionment, but to conventions.

6. There was no historical basis for the Dirksen assumption that one house of a legislature should be based on factors other than population.[23]

By the time the subcommittee concluded its hearings in June and prepared to consider the amendment, the effect of the lobbying and hearings was becoming noticeable. A "nose count" of senators taken in early June indicated that the Dirksen Amendment could be defeated if it remained in its present form. Also, Senator Dodd, a subcommittee member, was opposed to the amendment and Senator Bayh, who maintained impartiality throughout the hearings, stated that he could not accept the amendment as written. The Leadership Conference on Civil Rights—the coordinating group on civil rights legislation composed of ninety-five major organizations including the AFL-CIO and the NAACP—announced its opposition to the Dirksen Amendment and accepted the responsibility of lobbying against it.

[23] 111 *Congressional Record* 11848-61.

Nose counts in the House of Representatives indicated that the
amendment could be defeated there. The major problem was the
California Democratic delegation in the House. Since California
was under court order to redistrict its congressmen, anti-reapportionment legislators were attempting to exchange congressional support of the Dirksen amendment for a redistricting act favored by
the incumbent congressmen. The legislature adjourned, however,
without acting on either redistricting or reapportionment, thus
relieving the pressure.

In view of the improving outlook, fair representation leaders
decided to oppose any "improvements" in the Dirksen amendment
other than a change requiring it to be ratified by state conventions elected at large rather than by legislatures. This change was
proposed to highlight the popular sovereignty issue emphasized by
the sponsors of the amendment. Assuming they would reject the
change in ratification procedure, doubt could then be cast on their
sincerity in espousing popular sovereignty.

When the subcommittee met June 17, both Bayh and Dirksen
proposed new language. Bayh offered a substitute amendment which
was radically different from Dirksen's. His amendment first provided that state legislatures be based on population; next, as his
minimum price for support of an amendment, Bayh proposed that
only after a legislature had both its houses based on population
could it submit a non-population plan to the people. He carefully
circumscribed such a plan by providing that it might give "reasonable weight" only to geographic and political subdivision factors
in addition to "substantial equality of population." Finally, the
Bayh substitute required that the plan could be adopted no sooner
than the next election after an apportionment based on population
had occurred, and then only by a referendum. After each census,
any plan based on the other permissible factors would have to be
submitted to the voters for reapproval, and if rejected or not submitted, only a population apportionment would be permitted.
Bayh's substitute was defeated.

Dirksen offered to strike the first sentence of his original draft,
provide a means of periodic review of plans based on "other factors," and prohibit apportionments based on race, religion, or color.
When Senator Ervin objected to the latter amendment as an insult
to southern states, Dirksen withdrew it, saying he thought it un-
necessary.

Subsequently, the subcommittee reported a much revised amendment to the full judiciary committee by a vote of 5 to 3. As revised by Dirksen, the first sentence and the phrase "nothing in this constitution shall prohibit" were dropped, and a confusing and cumbersome section on periodic review was added. Non-population plans were to be re-submitted to the voters after each census. If approved, a plan remained in effect until changed, but if disapproved it could remain in effect for only two years or less until adoption of some other plan based on "other factors."

This version of the amendment attracted no new support. The primary objection to the periodic review section was that it allowed the legislature to submit the old system to the voters. This type of ratification of the status quo every ten years was one of the ways by which the reapportionment crisis had been created. Bayh opposed the changed amendment and Senator Javits, a member of the full Judiciary Committee, said he could not support it in that form. Javits was now particularly concerned about the civil rights implications of the amendment. Another factor relevant to his position was that he was the manager of John V. Lindsay's mayoralty campaign in New York City. Liberal party leaders, who had just endorsed Lindsay, were most unhappy with Javits' position in favor of an amendment to limit the one-man one-vote ruling. Javits' position had now become the key to committee action, however. Only he and Senator Hugh Scott (R., Pa.) remained undecided on their final course of action. If Javits voted with opponents of the Dirksen Amendment, the committee would split evenly, and lacking a majority, no report could be made to the Senate.

Dirksen now began to seek a better compromise to blunt criticism by civil rights advocates and to woo Javits and Bayh. He first tried to limit other factors to geography or political subdivisions, such as those specified by Bayh. Secondly, he limited the legislature to only one attempt at re-submission of the old formula, instead of two as in the subcommittee version. Bayh still insisted that the legislatures first be equally apportioned before another plan could be drawn, and Javits began to suggest that any amendment might be premature. He said that he felt it might be well to wait a few years to see whether an amendment were really necessary.[24]

In further efforts to obtain Javits' crucial support, Dirksen continued to modify his language to avoid the civil rights issue and to satisfy the periodic review problem. He could not modify too

[24] *Baltimore Sun,* June 29, 1964, p. 4.

greatly, however, without endangering his support from other senators on the Committee. On July 19, after a long period of hesitation,
Javits held a press conference to announce his decision. His "mature" judgment was to vote against the amendment unless the
courts were clearly given power to review the "reasonableness" of
plans using other factors. This Dirksen could not accept, since it
would virtually codify *Reynolds* and *Lucas* into the written constitution and leave the amendment with no practical effect.

When the Judiciary Committee met the following day, the eight
opponents of the amendment were present and ready to vote. But
all of Dirksen's supporters were not present. Dirksen was faced with
outright defeat rather than a mere tie. Senators Ervin, Smathers,
Scott, and McClellan were absent. So he filibustered by reading a
proposed report in order to postpone a vote. He suggested after
the meeting that he would still try to bring his resolution to the
floor.

Dirksen Strikes Out

The committee had met on Tuesday. On Thursday, Dirksen
made his move. As in his earlier effort with the foreign aid rider,
he would amend a bill already on the Senate floor. Because he now
proposed a constitutional amendment, however, he had to substitute the entire text of his amendment for the entire text of the
chosen bill, because a constitutional amendment requires a two-
thirds vote for passage rather than a simple majority. The problem was to find a suitable vehicle for the sacrifice, preferably another joint resolution.

Only one resolution was on the Senate calendar when Dirksen
decided on his tactic. S.J. Res. 66 provided that the week of August
31–September 6 be designated "National American Legion Baseball
Week." Dirksen, through the cooperation of Majority Leader Mansfield, moved to make this resolution the pending order of business.
Once he succeeded, he could offer his constitutional amendment as
a substitute for it.

The opposition forces, captained by Senator Paul Douglas, were
aware of Dirksen's intentions, but decided not to block Dirksen's
attempt to call up the baseball resolution. Their vote count indicated that they could defeat the Dirksen amendment in its present
form. Their greatest concern was that the astute Dirksen would

find language which might succeed in splitting their ranks. Thus, they prepared for what Douglas preferred to call a "discussion in depth."

A meeting of the staff members of senators opposing the amendment made plans for scheduling senators for the floor debate to insure that at least two opponents of the amendment were on the floor at all times. Debate topics were also outlined, and assignments made for the preparation of sufficient material to sustain senators for several weeks if the need arose. A new count of opponents was undertaken, and the senators, Vice-President Humphrey, and representatives of labor unions, the Fair Representation committee, and the Leadership Conference on Civil Rights accepted responsibilities for persuading uncommitted senators to vote with the Douglas group. Douglas prepared a "round robin," or petition, declaring opposition to the Dirksen amendment and began to collect senatorial signatures. This would give the opponents precise knowledge of their hard core strength. The strategy of the Douglas group was to obtain the votes to defeat the amendment as soon as possible, but to be prepared to debate indefinitely if the votes were not certain, or if Dirksen "sweetened" his proposal to attract more votes.

When Dirksen offered his motion to substitute, Douglas was ready. He labled Dirksen's motion "a foul ball." Aside from the ensuing duel in metaphors, however, the debate itself was relatively unimportant in determining the alignment of votes. It did, however, raise to public attention the conflicting political values embodied in the proposal. The debate also revealed a certain amount of confusion about the exact meaning and intent of the amendment. Javits, in offering his draft amendment as a substitute for the Dirksen version, emphasized that the latter deprived courts of jurisdiction in reapportionment cases by eliminating the standard of "reasonableness" from its text.

The debate proceeded sporadically for a week. At the first caucus, the Douglas group could count on the votes of at least thirty senators. By the end of the first week of debate they had collected twenty-six signatures and six unsigned pledges. In addition, they could count three more votes they considered "certain." They could then defeat the amendment in its present form. At this point, they, along with Dirksen, developed a unanimous consent agreement to vote on August 4, after six hours of debate. Douglas reserved the right to extend the debate if substantial changes were made in the amendment.

Among the undecided or uncommitted senators were Democrats Montoya, McIntyre, Muskie, Pell, Randolph, and Yarborough, and Republican Senator Caleb Boggs. By the weekend before the vote, McIntyre, Muskie, and Yarborough had committed themselves to oppose the amendment. Boggs, after prolonged hesitation and urging from friends in Delaware finally decided to oppose Dirksen. Hours before the vote Montoya and Randolph also joined the opposition, bringing the total strength of the Douglas forces to thirty-nine, since Senator Eugene McCarthy was hospitalized.[25] Two Dirksen supporters, Stuart Symington (D., Mo.) and Russell Long (D., La.), withheld their votes, however, in an agreement to "pair" with the absent McCarthy. Two votes in the affirmative were needed to match McCarthy because final passage required two-thirds.

Javits' substitute was defeated 85 to 12.[26] All other amendments except some word changes were rejected by voice votes. Douglas was ready to vote. The motion to substitute the Dirksen amendment for the baseball resolution carried by a vote of 59 to 39.[27] An hour later, the vote on final passage was 57 to 39.[28] The amendment failed, lacking a two-thirds majority. While Dirksen declaimed that he would not give up the fight, there was now no substantial hope that an amendment could pass the Congress. *Reynolds* v. *Sims* was still to be the law of the land.

The politics of constitutional change depends heavily upon the language used to symbolize the values that the change would establish as constitutional mandates. It also depends on the existence of wide agreement with those values, and on the patterns of behavior which may be anticipated as a result of the change. Disagreement on language represents a far deeper discord on values and politics. And such disagreement tends to defeat the challenge of existing constitutional law.

[25] It should be emphasized that this discussion is based on the way these senators were counted by the Douglas forces, and not on their personal attitudes. It is conceivable that their decisions were made earlier, but just not made publicly or counted by the people making the head count.

[26] 111 *Congressional Record* 18608-09 (August 4, 1965).

[27] 111 *Congressional Record* 18641-42 (August 4, 1965).

[28] 111 *Congressional Record* 18660 (August 4, 1965).

CONSTITUTIONAL DEMOCRACY: A POLITICAL THICKET

> *The true distinction between despotism and constitutional government does not lie in limitation of power but in the existence of a means for making power accountable for its behavior.*
>
> Henry Jones Ford
> *Representative Government,* 1924

> *. . . constitutional rules are not crucial, independent factors in maintaining democracy; rather, the rules themselves seem to be functions of underlying nonconstitutional factors.*
>
> Robert A. Dahl
> *A Preface to Democratic Theory,* 1956

The idea of equal representation in the legislature traveled a long and tortuous road from an imperative condition of John Locke's theory of representative government to the decision in *Reynolds* v. *Sims* and the defeat of the Dirksen Amendment. The distance between theory and constitution, and between constitution and politics may be great, but it is in the political thicket made from the intertwining of these three elements that a constitutional democracy must operate.

For a government to be both *constitutional* and *democratic* involves a certain amount of political tension. Both terms have special meaning to the way the system operates. The reapportionment controversy, which touches basic constitutional relationships and involves itself intimately in theories of democracy and representative government, focuses sharply on the interactions of theory, constitutional law, and politics in American constitutional democracy.

102

POLITICAL VALUES
AND CONSTITUTIONAL LAW

There are many theories of democracy. Our concern, however, is not with any one theory in particular, but with those common elements of democratic thought which converge in American culture to produce a group of widely accepted beliefs. This system of beliefs is generally referred to as the "democratic creed." Included in the creed are beliefs in the ideal of political equality, the doctrine of majority rule as a proper expression of popular sovereignty, the rights of individuals, the rule of law, and a sense of fair play. There is doubtless much wider agreement in these elements of the creed in the abstract than in specific applications of them. There is also considerable evidence that they are more widely accepted among the leadership strata of the political system than among the "followers." [1]

The democratic creed is significant, not as a coherent or systematic theory of democracy, but as "pop" theory, which has a favorable response when invoked in the politics of running a country. It provides many rules for the game of politics, roughs in the standards by which actions can be measured, and provides symbolic hooks on which to hang rationalizations for actions taken or proposed. The very vagueness of the concepts enhances their popularity.

In part growing from the democratic creed, but in part running parallel to it are the theories of representative government. All governments, to be sure, represent. All are not *representative*. Representative government is inextricably linked to the concepts of political equality and popular sovereignty. Its basic conditions include:

1. the consent of the governed, vesting actual control over government in the hands of the people through an official system of representation;

2. the accountability of the representatives to those affected by official decisions; and

[1] See Herbert McCloskey, "Issue Conflict and Consensus Among Party Leaders and Followers," *American Political Science Review*, LIV (1960), pp. 406-427. Also see Robert A. Dahl, *Who Governs?* (New Haven: Yale University Press, 1963), pp. 311-325.

3. the representativeness of the officials and publicly chosen institutions of their electorates.[2]

While each of these conditions is basic to a theory of representative government, all theories of representative government do not meet the conditions in the same way. While universal suffrage is now almost a universal rule in modern democracies, it was not always so. Some theories of representative government, therefore, limited those who gave consent to the propertied or to white men. Other theories, such as John C. Calhoun's concurrent majorities, or even the mixed government theories of John Adams or James Madison, found the basis for consent in the classes, orders, or "interests" of society rather than in individuals.

The purpose for which government exists determines the nature of the manner in which consent is given and officials are held accountable. A scheme of representation which might seem appropriate if government is to reflect individual opinions, promote individual liberty, or elevate the character of men by training them in statecraft, might be most ineffective in a system meant to limit governmental interference with the existing class and economic structure of society. This, too, is one conception of "liberty."

Each alternative purpose for a government raises questions about those entitled to representation in the government, the degree of equality among participants, the procedure by which decisions will be made, and the structure within which these decisions are reached. Depending upon the purposes of his system, a philosopher or politician might become an advocate of mixed government, bicameralism, federalism, plural voting, concurrent majorities, or proportional representation.

[2] These conditions are similar to those listed in Henry Jones Ford, *Representative Government* (New York: Henry Holt and Co., 1924), p. 158. Alfred A. De Grazia, *Apportionment and Representative Government* (New York: Frederick A. Praeger, 1963), p. 11, develops a different list, emphasizing constitutional restraints and access of various interests. His listing follows:

"a. A pervasive doctrine of the consent of the people as the basis of government.
b. Provision for entry of various kinds of opinions and interests into the political process and legislation.
c. Limits on the extent to which dissenting groups can be coerced.
d. A rule of law, applicable to government as well as the people."

I have no disagreement with this listing. Its points are subsumed in the one I have used or are developed in the discussions of the democratic creed and constitutionalism.

Each system favors certain people and interests over others. Each system is designed to be more "representative" of the interests entitled to a voice in the affairs of state, and thus to assure fulfillment of the purposes of representative government itself. As a corollary, each theory of representative government may be viewed as an attempt by its beneficiaries to rationalize the existing system, or as an attempt to change the rules for the distribution of power by those dissatisfied with the lot thrust upon them.

The particular brand of representative government employed fills in some of the blank spots in the democratic creed. It helps determine what is defined as a majority, or even "the" majority. It may create "minorities." The meaning of political equality becomes a little more precise as access to the political process is expanded or limited by the mechanics of representation such as apportionment, districting, and voting.

Certain values from the democratic creed and theories of representative government such as equality, popular sovereignty, consent, and majority rule, if left standing alone, could make democracy appear to be little more than an exercise in stacking the meeting. A majority of those who vote or legislate exercise the sovereignty. The task of politics is to accumulate the greater number of equal participants.

Other values from the democratic creed of representative government also interpose on this simple design. Concepts of minority and individual rights, accountability, fair play, and the rule of law propose to limit the inclination of a majority to act arbitrarily or to tyrannize those who do not approve of majority sentiments. But these values are only arguments to be voted down by the majority unless they occupy a special place in the government. They must be translated from the realm of political theory, creed, or argument into constitutional limitations and constitutional law.

A constitution and constitutional law are an exercise in the goring of oxen. When a constitutional provision is written, amended, or modified by practice or interpretation, some political values are chosen over others; some interests are served better than others. In the form of constitutional law, *natural* rights which were formerly arguments against abuse of authority became *civil* rights or liberties which are enforceable by the authority of the state itself.

A constitution and constitutional law in establishing a particular representative system chooses among competing values, concepts, and definitions. In this light, constitutional law consists of a series of value mandates which officials are supposed to follow or observe.

Because constitutions are writen by politicians and not by philosophers, the values embodied in a constitution are often vaguely stated, or only implicit. It often becomes necessary to expand upon, interpret, or justify a constitutional provision. This exercise may require the development of new values. A new theory of bicameral representation developed, for example, to justify the scheme of representation employed in the Congress, which initially sprung from no theory at all but from the need for a workable compromise. And the developing practice of judicial review was justified by adaptation of pre-revolutionary constitutional theory. As the rationalizations for the "federal plan" of representation and for judicial review hardened into doctrine, both could be used in subsequent controversies which sought to have the courts, as the authoritative exponent of constitutional law under the doctrine of judicial review, make a choice among possible value mandates on state bicameralism.

In its selection of values, constitutional law does not uniformly adhere to the most favored tenets of the democratic creed. The framers of a constitution may very well stack the legislature to favor interests they prefer over others. They very well may qualify access to the political processes. This may not be "democratic." Slavery was not democratic, for instance, but it was constitutional. Slavery could persist, however, until the political support for the values of emancipation forced a confrontation between the constitutional law of slavery and the ethic of freedom. In this case, the respective strength of the contenders of reform and stasis were such that civil war resulted. As one result of the conflict, the constitutional law of the *Dred Scott* decision gave way to the values of emancipation, citizenship, and equal access to the political processes embodied in the Thirteenth, Fourteenth, and Fifteenth Amendments to the Constitution.

The Fourteenth Amendment particularly reflects the politics of uncertain and imprecise value choices. Its values had to be interpreted to form a body of enforceable constitutional law. And the history of the Due Process Clause alone amply illustrates the historical interplay of constitutional law with political and economic thought.[3]

When a clash occurs between the existing constitutional law of the system, and the demand for recognition of widely accepted polit-

---

[3] See especially John R. Commons, *Legal Foundations of Capitalism* (Madison: University of Wisconsin Press, 1957).

ical values, some means of reconciliation must be found. A variety of means are available. Amendment has already been mentioned as one way of reconciling the constitution to political values. But new political values may also give way to the constitution. Either by failure of amendments or by interpretation of officials (primarily courts), political values may fail to become constitutional law. In some instances they may be declared unconstitutional. The concept of federalism which supported secession of states, for instance, was declared unconstitutional,[4] as was the idea that a state might require children to salute the flag as a means of developing patriotism.[5] Or, the constitution may be interpreted to incorporate a political value, thus changing the substance of the constitution while leaving its language intact. Through this method the school desegregation problem was handled, as were earlier problems of national supremacy and economic regulation.

It also is important to understand that the sort of decisions discussed here are rarely clear-cut. Frequently more than one value is involved. The values of majority rule or of legislative discretion may conflict with values of fair play or individual rights. And it is not easy to challenge established constitutional law, which represents a political value in the first place chosen by a tedious process of drafting and ratification or interpretation. Moreover, the Constitution and its integrity as the embodiment of the best political wisdom of the culture has a value in itself. Ours is a nation of constitution worshipers. An evil may frequently be long and cheerfully endured if it is a constitutional evil.

Constitutionalism, as an ingredient in the value system of a constitutional democracy, not only prescribes the rules of the game, establishes substantive privileges, and organizes the system of government, it also operates as a brake on alteration of the law of the constitution and tends to force dissension over political values into a debate over which set of values best preserves the "true" meaning of the Constitution. No politician hoping for success attacks the Constitution—only its usurpation, non-enforcement, or misinterpretation.

By a combination of custom, abdication by the other branches of the government, and judicial practice, the national judiciary—especially the Supreme Court—has become the principal protector of the Constitution and of the concepts of constitutionalism. These con-

---

[4] *Texas* v. *White,* 7 Wall. 700 (1869).
[5] *Board of Education* v. *Barnette,* 319 U.S. 624 (1943).

cepts, as practiced in conjunction with the democratic creed, have inculcated values concerning the proper role of the court in a constitutional democracy. And just as there is disagreement over the values the Constitution should support, there is extensive disagreement over the role the Court should play in the political system. As a result, the Court, in the cases which come before it, and at different periods in its history, moves from one role to another.

The major portion of the Court's business is not particularly controversial. When it acts to clarify the statute and case law in non-constitutional areas, or when it performs its central role in the administration of the federal court system, its decisions are only rarely subjected to searching public debate. It is in its political role that controversy flares, as it has throughout its history.[6]

The political role played in a particular era, or even in a given case, is determined by the members of the Court, the circumstances of the case, and the political environment of the time. The Court may, as in *Colegrove,* decide to avoid the issue entirely, using the political question doctrine or invoking the concept of equitable restraint. In many cases in its history, the Court has not hesitated actively to assert its judgment on the substance of legislation in preference to that of the legislature. But in more recent years, it has tended to make strong assumptions in favor of the constitutionality of legislation. But at the same time the Vinson and Warren courts in particular have tended to review carefully any interference with "preferred freedoms"—those cases which (1) might involve a direct violation of the Bill of Rights or an indirect violation through state action proscribed by the Fourteenth Amendment; (2) involve a restriction of access to the political process; and (3) involve laws directed against any insular minority so subject to prejudice that it has no real voice in the political process.[7]

---

[6] For an excellent discussion of the major roles of the Court, see Robert H. Jackson, *The Supreme Court in the American System of Government* (Cambridge, Mass.: Harvard University Press, 1955). Also cf. Victor G. Rosenblum, *Law as a Political Instrument* (New York: Random House, 1955) and Jack Peltason, *The Federal Courts in the Political Process* (New York: Random House, 1955).

[7] These ideas first appeared in a footnote by Mr. Chief Justice Harlan F. Stone in *U.S.* v. *Caroline Products,* 304 U.S. 144 (1938). For an excellent discussion of the use of these doctrines in the reapportionment and other civil liberties cases by the Warren Court, see Walter F. Murphy, "Deeds Under a Doctrine: Civil Liberties in the 1963 Term," *American Political Science Review* LIX (March 1965), 72-79.

In political perspective, the court may act either as a ratifier or limiter and nullifier of the acts of electoral or legislative majorities. In this role it asserts the value of constitutionality in competition with the value of majority rule. The court also acts in this capacity as an instrument of constitutional adjustment, interpreting the constitution to conform with the policies of the government or the consensus among the nation's leaders on the practical needs of the country. Where the court has stood in defiance of the rest of the government, it has eventually either had to retreat, or found its decisions unenforced. None of the more forceful presidents has hesitated to "pack" a Supreme Court or the whole federal judiciary in the hope of producing decisions congenial to his policy objectives.

THE POLITICS
OF CONSTITUTIONAL DEMOCRACY

It is in the context of the relationship of values to constitutional law that the reapportionment battle assumes extra significance as an illustration of the way a constitutional democracy works in resolving fundamental political problems. At different stages of the reapportionment battle, the contestants used different values as tools in advancing their cases politically or legally.

The initial value mandates for apportionment and representative systems were chosen by conventions which wrote the state constitutions, or by subsequent amendments developed through the political process. Some states, like Tennessee, chose the value of one-man one-vote as the basic mandate for apportioning. Others, like Delaware, either chose no value at all in preference to a bald allocation based only on power to decide, or chose values which weighted the representation of some citizens heavier than others, in order to protect favored "interests" in the state. Such systems could rely on the values of fair play and minority rights for justification. And more recent maneuvers such as those in Illinois and Michigan, while reflecting the existing distribution of power in state politics, could rely on the value of mixed representation.

These values were not self-executing in all instances. Certainly they were rigorously followed in some states, where perpetuation of the value was also congenial to the existing system of power. But in other states the constitutional mandates were ignored. In either case, the practical politics of the system shaped the effective meaning of the constitution. And in either case, political values were used by both the opponents and proponents of the resulting apportionment to attack and defend the system. Where the state constitution mandated one-man one-vote as the apportionment rule, the reformers could combine their values with a plea for constitutionalism. Where the constitution itself offended the preferred values, its change was urged to bring it into conformity with the favored interpretation of the democratic creed.

As value weapons, the reformers selected or emphasized particular elements of the democratic creed. They asserted first the concept of political equality and its counterpart of individual rights. These combined nicely to condemn any system which debased individual equality as the foundation of the political system or denied any person the basic "right" of equal access to the political process through the exercise of his suffrage. Secondly, the reformers were advocates of majority rule and went to great lengths to demonstrate the statistical impossibility (given their categories of urban vs. rural) of the majority of the population electing a majority of the legislatures. Given this demonstration, they argued that the basic conditions of representative government for consent of the governed and accountability to the electorate could not be met. They also attempted to illustrate the consequences of electoral discrimination appearing in their taxes and in programs affecting their problems. Their inability to obtain political redress violated the fair play tenet of the democratic creed. For the reformers, the key issue was one of representativeness. Their political system was one whose purpose was reflection of the popular will and advancement of the individual through equal participation in government. With such assumptions "no prejudices," in Jefferson's phrase, could justify an apportionment system not based on population. Representative institutions based on values other than one-man one-vote just were not "representative."

> . . . in the light of democratic principles, of history and of contemporary political theory, the only legitimate basis of representation in a state legislature is people. One man's vote must be worth the same as another's.[8]

The existing apportionments were not without defense, as we have already seen. Their defenders could rely first of all on the con-

---

[8] *One Man-One Vote,* Conference of Research Scholars and Political Scientists, Anthony Lewis, ed. (New York: Twentieth Century Fund, 1962), p. 3.

cept of constitutionalism. The issue had been adjudicated, after a fashion, and it was determined that reapportionment was one of those sensitive questions of political judgment best left to the political organs of government, and the political organs had made a considered judgment that the public interest was best served by implementing the value of mixed representation. All important interests were reflected in government. The act of compromise was encouraged, the system was more truly "representative" of the significant elements which made the state what it is, and the rights of minorities are insured against tyrannical behavior by the majority. Balanced representation was buttressed by the folklore of the federal analogy. Bicameralism, itself a value of considerable prestige, depended on a system in which one house represented other factors than population.

In a nonconstitutional system, and it seemed in a constitutional one as well, the values preferred by the defenders of the old apportionments would prevail. They could be sustained by the exercise of power alone. The reformers, by their own demonstrations, were permanently precluded from attaining enough power to change the stack of the meeting.

In the American constitutional system, however, what may be interpreted as a struggle for the power or a struggle for a substantive right, such as equal access to public schools, can be converted from a simple contest for popular favor or political power into a constitutional issue. The purpose of conversion is to make those who exercise power justify their acts, not just as "representative" or even as the will of the majority, but as *constitutional*. For the reformers, this meant translation of their preferred values into concepts of constitutional law which could be accepted either as an amendment or as case law by the Supreme Court. For the defenders of the system, conversion of the problem into a constitutional issue meant a need to justify their behavior in terms consistent with constitutional concepts. For both groups, choices were available.

The reformers chose as their vehicle one of the constitution's most malleable phrases, "equal protection of the laws." Their task, outlined earlier in this book, was to convince the Court that equal protection required individual equality of access to the political process through equal representation in the legislature and equal participation in statewide elections. Thus, they developed a theory of equal protection to cover their full objective of equal representation in both houses of the legislature: The Fourteenth Amendment protects *individuals* against state action. Reapportionment laws are state action, as it applies to either house. Equal protection demands that legislation have a permissible objective. Representation of all the people is the only permissible objective of an apportionment system. No other policy is rational in a democratic system. No classifications of people can be permitted which dilute some votes. All people must stand as equals in respect to representation. Representation is, thus, a personal right, and may not be diluted in one house, or in either. The value of individual rights forms the base of the argument. But assumptions of democratic theory underlie the entire construction.

The legislatures' defenders relied on constitutional values more than on alternative democratic theories. They had some difficulty in accommodating their systems with the more popular elements of the democratic creed such as equality and majority rule. Their defense was first to assert the then prevailing constitutional doctrine that reapportionment was a political question. It of necessity meant reconciling interests. This involved pragmatic compromise rather than legal logic. This led to choosing definitions of rationality drawn from economic regulation cases rather than civil rights and liberties cases. By analogy with these cases, legislative judgments should not be overturned. If any state of facts could be produced to justify the pattern, it should meet the rationality tests of equal protection. In essence, the defenders argued that anything devised by the legislature could be rational, if it actually did what they wanted it to do. As one enthusiast for the old New York apportionment system put it:

. . . in apportionment rationality is an ensemble of different permissible motives incorporated in a set of devices to assign seats to various groupings of a population.[9]

This generous interpretation of the rationality test of equal protection seemed behind the arguments of the Maryland attorney general that Baltimore was entitled to six senators for its million people, but Baltimore County only to one for its half million. Baltimore, it was argued, had a port, a factor which made the allocation rational. And Virginia justified its apportionment peculiarities by arguing that they could have resulted from subtraction of military personnel from census figures for certain populous areas.

The most urgent argument of the defenders, however, was on the

[9] Alfred De Grazia, *Apportionment and Representative Government* (New York: Alfred A. Knopf, Inc., 1951), p. 53.

bicameral question. After *Baker,* most defenders forsook even a pretense of justifying malapportionment in both houses of the legislatures. Some rather sophisticated arguments could be made for the rationality of bicameral systems with one house based at least partially, if not entirely, on non-population factors. One such argument (though it was not made before the Court) pointed out the need to distinguish representation as a process of political action and decision from the problem of weighting votes in elections. The second house, the argument ran, could be used to assure a voice for all significant interests in the state.[10] Such a system could be sustained as rational under the doctrines of equal protection if it allowed majority rule and required only a demonstration that a coherent pattern was followed. Rationality required a little flexibility. Equal protection should not be held to embrace only one political philosophy. The sophisticated arguments were not used in court, however. Instead, the defense of bicameralism rested largely on the readily refutable myth of the federal analogy and on the specious suggestion that if the courts struck down federal plans in the states under the equal protection clause, they might have to declare the U.S. Senate unconstitutional also.[11]

The most formidable problem for the reformers was the problem of jurisdiction of the courts. A theory had to be developed to justify judicial involvement and the courts must be convinced of the necessity of their intervention. Essentially the reformers pleaded with the Court to take action to prevent the destruction of democratic values. These values were equated with the doctrine of constitutionalism, which prohibits the arbitrary and unjust exercise of power.

The Court, then, was confronted first of all with the problem of choosing its own role in a constitutional democracy. It had at least three principal alternatives. It could confirm the Frankfurter political question doctrine and permanently foreclose the matter from judicial attention. This would, doubtless, have been the most convenient decision, and one immensely popular with legislators and many judges on the lower courts.

Secondly, the Court could have taken the escape favored by Mr.

[10] Robert G. Dixon, Jr., "Apportionment Standards and Judicial Power," 28 *Notre Dame Lawyer* 367. See pp. 386-91.
[11] For an example of the rationale of this position, see *Brief on Behalf of Appellees, Maryland Committee for Fair Representation* v. *Tawes* (Supreme Court of the United States, No. 29, October Term, 1963), pp. 38-42.

Justice Rutledge, and have said the question was justiciable, but that the cause of justice would not be served by deciding it. This seemed untenable due to the number of other cases moving toward the Court.

The Court actually took the third option, and accepted jurisdiction and proceeded to decide other cases on their merits. In so deciding, the Court accepted a role as protector of constitutional values. Specifically, the Court chose to follow its role of reading the Constitution as a democratic document. In so doing, it would allow a wide range for legislative action. But in presuming the constitutionality of legislation, it had a special burden to insure that the political process is actually democratic.[12] And it chose an active role in adjusting the Constitution to accommodate widespread sentiment. Important as evidence of this sentiment was the intervention of the solicitors general of both Republican and Democratic administrations. Their essential message to the Court was that there was consensus among the nation's parties and leaders that reapportionment of legislatures on a population basis was "in the national interest" and would be acceptable public policy.

To this role, Mr. Justice Harlan strenuously objected, along with Mr. Justice Frankfurter. Dissenting in *Reynolds*, Harlan scorned the view that:

> . . . every major social ill in this country can find its cure in some constitutional "principle," and that this Court should "take the lead" in promoting reform when other branches of the government fail to act. The Constitution is not a panacea for every blot upon the public welfare, nor should this Court, ordained as a judicial body, be thought of as a general haven for reform movements.[13]

As it moved from its first value choice of role to play to the second value choice of the constitutional basis for apportionment, the Court assumed the role of protecting democratic values through constitutional law decisions. The Court had alternative choices among democratic values. A majority chose egalitarian and majoritarian values. In the opinion in *Reynolds*, the chief justice delineates the aspects of the democratic creed and of the theory of representative government which underlay the decision.

> As long as ours is a representative form of government, and our legislatures are those instruments of government elected directly by and

[12] See Murphy, "Deeds Under a Doctrine," *op. cit.*, pp. 73ff.
[13] *Reynolds* v. *Sims*, 377 U.S. 533, 624-25, Mr. Justice Harlan dissenting.

directly representative of the people, the right to elect legislators in a free and unimpaired fashion is the bedrock of our political system.[14]

For Mr. Chief Justice Warren, representative government required "full and effective participation in the political processes" for every citizen. This requires equality in the election of representatives—a majority of people should be able to elect a majority of legislators. Minorities are protected by the Constitution against majority abuse.[15]

> . . . [T]he basic principle of representative government remains, and must remain, unchanged—the weight of a citizen's vote cannot be made to depend on where he lives.[16]

Justices Clark and Stewart would have followed a less rigorous philosophy than the chief justice. Mr. Justice Clark would not have applied the one-man one-vote principle arbitrarily to both houses, so long as a reasonable basis for departures from equality could be produced.[17]

Mr. Justice Stewart, also dissenting against the one-man one-vote principle, stated that he "could not join in the fabrication of a constitutional mandate which imparts and forever freezes one theory of political thought in our Constitution . . ." [18] He then, in essence, proposed his own philosophy of representative government and evolved a corresponding constitutional rule. For Stewart,

> Representative government is a process of accommodating group interests through democratic institutional arrangements. Its function is to channel the numerous opinions, interests, and abilities of the people of a State into the making of public policy. Appropriate legislative apportionment, therefore, should ideally be designed to insure effective representation in the state legislature, in cooperation with other organs of political power, of the various groups making up the electorate.[19]

Only two constitutional rules were required: (1) an apportionment plan must be rational "in the light of the State's own characteristics . . ." and (2) the plan must not "permit the systematic

[14] 377 U.S. 533, 562.
[15] 377 U.S. 533, 565-66.
[16] 377 U.S. 533, 567.
[17] *Lucas* v. *Colorado*, 377 U.S. 713, 741-43, Mr. Justice Clark dissenting.
[18] *WMCA* v. *Lomenzo*, 377 U.S. 633, 748, Mr. Justice Stewart dissenting.
[19] 377 U.S. 633, 749.

frustration of the will of the majority of the electorate of the State," [20]

The Court decided. It reconciled the Constitution as the majority of the Court understood it with the democratic creed as understood by them. Values were selected concerning the role of the Court and the mandate of the Constitution on apportionment. By avoiding at least for a time questions such as gerrymandering, and by using equal protection concepts instead of reversing the political question doctrine directly and interpreting the Guaranty Clause in Article IV, the Court did not develop a full theory of representative government. It assumed a series of values in mandating one particular concept of representativeness.

The result was not inevitable. With a different court, or with the same court under different circumstances or leadership, the Frankfurter opinion in *Colegrove* might have been confirmed, or the Clark or Stewart approaches chosen over the Warren approach. In any event, there was no possibility of a "neutral" decision. Judicial abstention would only permit one system of values to predominate. The Court decided to break the impasse of which John Locke spoke. The legislatures, which alone apparently had the power, refused to implement the values on which they were ostensibly based. The Court assumed the function Locke assigned his executive,

> . . . observing rather the true proportion than fashion of representation, [it] regulates not by custom but true reason the number of members . . . it being the interest as well as the intention of the people to have a fair and equal representative, whoever brings it nearest to that is an undoubted friend to, and establisher of the government and cannot miss the consent and approbation of the community. . . . Whatsoever shall be done manifestly for the good of the people, and the establishing the government upon its true foundations, is, and always will be, just prerogative.[21]

The test of the Court's opinion, however, was not in its logic or conformity to either the democratic creed or the canons of judicial behavior or the folklore of constitutionalism. The real test was in its acceptance as a value mandate of representative government; in its durability as enforceable constitutional law; in its capacity to survive the political thicket in which it was born. Survival depended primarily on political forces outside the Court.

[20] 377 U.S. 633, 753-54.
[21] John Locke, *Second Treatise of Civil Government* (1689), par. 158.

The political climate appeared to be sufficient for survival, if not entirely cordial. The decision itself set in motion new political activities by both reformers and defenders. An announcement by a court that it has reached a decision does not terminate the life of an issue. It may only intensify debate and conflict by breaking the inertia which contained the contest prior to the decision. The bench and the hustings are not antithetical forums. They are different stages for the continuing debates of democratic government.

The new rules of the game, first of all, redistributed political resources. The authority of constitutionalism and the Court now stood on the side of the reformers. Judicial injunctions were now available to force change. The exact nature of the change, however, still rested with the old regimes. The decision placed limits on politics through deadlines and standards. So the emphasis in preservation of the status quo changed from brazen displays of power to more subtle forms and formulas of apportionment, to delay, and finally to an attempt to nullify the decision by constitutional amendment.

The Court's action also performed an educative function in that it placed the prestige of the Court on the side of one approach to representative government in preference to others. While this did not immediately result in acceptance of its doctrines by the defenders of the old system, the decision had a sufficient impact on opinion to narrow significantly the permissible bounds of conflict. After the decision there developed little support for use of nonpopulation factors in both houses. Debate was limited to senates. And by 1965, even those unhappy with the decision seemed ready to concede the propriety of judicial review over one house, even limiting their objections to elimination of review in the second house only if a plan were approved in a referendum.

Contestants in the battle also emphasized different values in appealing for political support after the court decisions. The proponents of the Dirksen Amendment utilized the value of popular sovereignty by arguing for a concept of direct consent through referendum as the hallmark of popular sovereignty and majority rule. They still championed the cause of "the" minority and envisioned a tyranny of the majority if the Supreme Court ruling were left intact. While the early phases of the debates on the 1963 Council of State Governments amendments, the Dirksen rider, and the Tuck bill dwelt on a judicial restraint role for the courts, this value tended to disappear as a major theme in their discussions by 1965.

Dirksen's opponents—the reformers—now became proponents

of the new constitutional *status quo,* and emphasized constitutional values previously denied them, particularly those which asserted representation to be a right of an individual protected against the action of any majority, legislative or popular. They countered Dirksen's argument for direct consent with the value of consent through representation, thus requiring equal participation in election of representatives as well as in referendums. Finally, the opponents of the Dirksen Amendment adhered to the values of individual and minority rights in making their case that it would allow discrimination against Negroes in southern state politics and against urban minorities in other states.

The problem for the Dirksen forces which could not be resolved was to reconcile their constitutional proposals with enough accepted tenets of the democratic creed. Not only was there now an official restatement of the application of that creed to the apportionment issue, but the inertia of the system had been reversed. As each court decision was implemented, and each legislature reapportioned, the official value mandate of constitutional law was joined by a redistribution of political power and a shift of pressure which tended to reinforce that mandate.

By late 1965, well over one-fourth plus one of the states needed to block ratification of a constitutional amendment had legislatures, or would soon have them, with vested interests in preserving the one-man one-vote rule. The system was reaching a new state of repose in which its politics could be justified both by the tests of constitutional law and the democratic creed. A new consensus seemed in the making as a result of the court decisions, actual reapportionments, and the failure of the Dirksen Amendment. Equal representation seemed due for status as an accepted doctrine in American government. That this seemed so should not be taken, however, to suggest that it would be an immutable law of the American political system. Times change, and with them the acceptability of old doctrines of democratic government and constitutional law. Witness the demise of the separate-but-equal doctrine in the field of Negro rights.

The lesson is that in a constitutional democracy it is quite possible that practices will develop which are sanctioned, as was malapportionment, either by overt design or by omission of constitutional law, even though these practices do not conform either to philosophical or popular conceptions of democracy. It is also possible that practices will develop or be advocated which seem to be democratic, but are proscribed by the applied constitution. And it is conceivable that power might be exercised which is sanctioned neither by democratic *nor* constitutional values.

That which distinguishes the politics of constitutional democracy from raw politics or even plain constitutional politics is the constant political need in such a system to justify the uses of power. Power must be rationalized both on constitutional grounds and for its own consistency within the democratic creed. When it cannot meet both tests, the legitimacy of its acts becomes questionable. An act must be not only democratic; it must be constitutional. When the dual test does not pass general satisfaction, the issue then must be resolved either by adjusting the value to accommodate the practice, or adjusting the constitution to accommodate the value. And in response to either, the political process reacts by acquiescence or by an attempt at further change.

Constitutional democracy is not simply institutions, constitutions, philosophical logic, or political experience alone. Rather it involves a constant interaction among these forces which represent, reflect, and shape human behavior.[22]

[22] See Thomas L. Thorson, *The Logic of Democracy* (New York: Holt, Rinehart and Winston, Inc., 1962).

THE FUTURE OF
REPRESENTATIVE GOVERNMENT:
A VIEW FROM THE THICKET

> *"The new age of human relationships"*
> *has no political agencies worthy of it. The*
> *democratic public is still largely inchoate*
> *and unorganized.*
>
> John Dewey
> *The Public and Its Problems,* 1927

> *The organization of consent is the great-*
> *est problem of our day.*
>
> C. E. Merriam
> *Prologue to Politics,* 1939

With the failure of the Dirksen Amendment, the last critical phase in the conflict over the basis of legislative apportionment came to an end. The value mandate of one-man one-vote was sustained. But this by no means resolved all questions about the character of representative government in American constitutional democracy. Now there was an official position on apportionment. But there was no official decision—or even much public discussion —about the best system of representation for modern American government.

The New Constitutional Law
of Fair Representation

Reynolds v. *Sims,* its companions, and its progeny remained a narrow decision in spite of its thunderous impact on state legislatures. It established a rule only for that aspect of the concept of

120

representativeness that deals with the apportionment of legislators. *Wesberry* v. *Sanders* and *Sanders* v. *Gray* carried only the one-man one-vote doctrine to congressional elections and to statewide elections, respectively. The *per curiam* decisions of 1965 elaborated the rulings no further than in the original opinions.

While the new meaning of Equal Protection received no immediate extension by the Court, the outlines of new politico-constitutional problems began to unfold. First of all was the gerrymander. The Court had avoided this problem in *Wright* v. *Rockefeller* when it upheld a New York federal court ruling that the plaintiffs had not proved that Manhattan congressional districts had been drawn from motives of racial discrimination. In other words, the Court held that there was no proof of overt racial discrimination in the construction of the districts as there had been in the redrawing of the municipal boundaries of Tuskegee in *Gomillion* v. *Lightfoot*. The opinion would seem to confirm *Gomillion's* ruling that overt racial gerrymanders are unconstitutional under the Fifteenth Amendment.

Because the case was disposed of on the question of proof, the gerrymander issue was not explored in much detail. In their dissents, Justices Douglas and Goldberg did deal with the problem of racial gerrymandering. Mr. Justice Douglas in particular emphasized his belief that no defense whatever could justify a racial gerrymander which separates races into separate districts. He rejected the idea that race could be a criterion in districting, even if it could be shown to result in the election to office of members of that race who otherwise could not be elected. Specifically asserting that the Fourteenth Amendment, in light of the school desegregation cases, prohibited racial segregation in the public arena,[1] he wrote:

> The fact that Negro political leaders find advantage in this nearly Negro and Puerto Rican district is irrelevant to our problem. Rotten boroughs were long a curse of democratic processes. Racial boroughs are also at war with democratic standards.[2]

The important point for this discussion is Douglas' political theory of the Fourteenth Amendment. It requires equality of the

[1] *Wright* v. *Rockefeller*, 376 U.S. 52, 62, Mr. Justice Douglas dissenting (italics his).
[2] 376 U.S. 52, 62.

individual. Douglas holds with Goldberg, who concluded that "The Fourteenth Amendment commands equality, and racial segregation by law is inequality." [3] In Douglas' words:

> . . . the individual is important, not his race. The principle of equality is at war with the notion that District A must be represented by a Negro, as it is with the notion that District B must be represented by a Caucasian, District C by a Jew, District D by a Catholic, and so on. . . . That system, by whatever name it is called, is a devisive force in the community, emphasizing differences between candidates and voters that are irrelevant in the constitutional sense.[4]

Douglas recognized that race and religion play roles in political choices. "But government has no business designing electoral districts along racial or religious lines." He would allow it only if the unit represented an actual neighborhood. To do otherwise, he argued, would divide groups "the constitution seeks to weld together as one" and such districts would "seek not the best representative but the best racial or religious partisan. Since that system is at war with the democratic ideal, it should find no footing here." [5]

The Douglas dissent contains a rather full interpolation of the democratic creed into the Equal Protection Clause. If ultimately accepted by the majority of the Court as a proper union of *Reynolds* and *Gomillion* in meeting the gerrymander problem, it would emphatically commit the Court to the elimination of both overt and covert racial gerrymandering. It could even suggest that a state must be ready to prove that any racially homogeneous legislative district is an almost inevitable consequence of the use of purely population or neighborhood considerations. Manageable standards for evaluating such data are not readily available. What is a neighborhood? If districts are compact and equally populous, are they racially discriminatory if they are homogeneous or heterogeneous in ethnic composition? [6]

While the racial gerrymander poses a difficult constitutional problem in the perspective of *Gomillion* and even *Wright* v.

---

[3] 376 U.S. 52, 69, Mr. Justice Goldberg, dissenting.
[4] 376 U.S. 52, 66, Mr. Justice Douglas, dissenting.
[5] 376 U.S. 52, 67.
[6] For a thorough discussion of the problems of minority group and minority party representation, see Malcolm E. Jewell, "Minority Representation: A Political or Judicial Question," 53 *Kentucky Law Journal* 267 (1964-65).

Rockefeller, the really difficult problem is the nonracial gerrymander, usually directed against the minority party in the legislature or against an economic or social interest, or against a jurisdiction. Districts of equal population which are even symmetrical may
be devised which grossly disadvantage one political party or the
"urbanist" interests of a central city. By quartering a city entitled
to one district and dividing it among four districts, three fourths
of each of the constituencies would be comprised of suburban or
rural voters. If the urban and suburban parties differed, the urban
party would probably suffer virtual electoral extinction. So might
any organic interests in finance or legislation that the city might
have as a jurisdiction.

The one-man one-vote mandate is scrupulously followed. Any
hint of racial segregation is avoided. But is a potential majority
party or majority interest prevented from becoming a majorty? In
all likelihood the answer must be "yes." Even so, how can the principle of majority rule be converted into a workable bit of constitutional law without preventing legitimate and very useful division
of jurisdictions or interests into separate districts? There is no suggestion that the problem is one the courts cannot resolve. But resolution will be difficult in the absence of any clearer theoretical
guidelines than presently exist. Neither political leaders nor the
courts seem presently inclined toward proportional representation as
a required constitutional means of resolving such a dilemma, although P.R. remains one practicable political alternative. Some
writers feel that this problem will be insignificant. Once the population standard must be met, they feel no "outrageous" advantages
will accrue to the majority party. Thus, there is no need to develop
a constitutional standard for the shape or partisan "neutrality" of
districts.[7]

The history of the gerrymander as a creative art, however, suggests some caution at so sanguine a view.[8] A few other devices illustrate the point and the problem of devising all-encompassing constitutional standards to meet the more imaginative forms of chi-
canery in the politics of representation.

One case which offers a complex, but nonetheless important
problem in fair representation has already been dismissed by the

[7] Andrew Hacker, *Congressional Redistricting* (Washington: The Brookings
Institution, 1963), p. 120. See pp. 46-53 for a discussion of the varieties of
gerrymandering.
[8] See Jewell, "Minority Representation," *op. cit.,* 271-86.

Supreme Court.[9] South Carolina's House of Representatives is elected from multi-member districts, each sending three or more representatives to the state house. There is no problem of constitutionality in multi-member districts, as such. But the election law requires that a voter, to cast a valid ballot in such a legislative race, must vote for as many representatives as that district is allotted.

This system places an almost insurmountable hardship on the minority party and on the minority faction of the dominant party in the primary. In such districts the minority can often assure itself representation by bullet voting—casting only one vote for a single minority candidate. Thus, if no minority party member votes for a majority party candidate, and a few majority voters cross the ballot, the least popular majority candidate will lose to the minority's selection.

This is not permitted in South Carolina.[10] To have his vote counted for his preferred candidate, the minority voter must either cast two votes for candidates he opposes, thus almost guaranteeing they will both have a higher vote than the one he prefers, or he must waste two votes by writing in the names of other persons. Of course, a full slate could run to represent the minority except that this is often impossible to accomplish, and it tends to scatter the vote, making somewhat less probable the election of any one minority representative.

The impact of this system was examined using the actual case of a district electing ten representatives. There was a full slate of Democrats, but only two Republicans on the ballot. Simulation of the election on a computer revealed that for a single Republican to be elected, eighty-three per cent of all voters would have to cast their votes for him, while any of the ten Democrats could be elected with only fifty-one per cent of the votes.[11]

Such a system has grand possibilities for reducing minority party and factional influence in state politics. Where factions are based on race, it would seem to raise serious constitutional questions. Not only does such a system debase the value of the vote, and even refuse to count a vote as cast, it raises what may ultimately be as

[9] *Boineau* v. *Thornton*, 379 U.S. 15 (1964).
[10] There are similar statutes in Louisiana and North Carolina.
[11] *Boineau* v. *Thornton*, Civil Action No. AC-1465, U.S. District Court, Eastern District of South Carolina, Petitioners Complaint, Appendix A (June 27, 1964).

large an issue as apportionment itself: is the vote a form of political expression? If it is, then must the Constitution protect not only the right to register that expression but also the right to withhold a vote—as a corollary means of effective expression? These were the questions raised by the South Carolina case for which no answers were available.

The districting system may also be mixed to produce exquisite constitutional problems. Districts may be created using a formula based on the average population per representative. Rural districts will, under such a system, elect one representative; more densely populated districts will elect two or more. Such districts may apparently be created by any nonracial design. Counties might be combined or divided as the fancy of the districting authority dictates. The dominant party or faction in the multi-member districts will tend to benefit from such an arrangement. Some ethnic minorities will find that in spite of this new political equality, when they are lumped into mammoth districts their influence as groups on the selection of representatives is reduced. Fourteen senators elected from fourteen districts will be different senators from fourteen elected at large. Such plans can be defended, however, as requiring area-wide perspectives on legislation instead of encouraging narrow parochialism. Single-member districts in urban areas may only entrench local political organizations in control of one-party ghettos. But multi-member districts encompassing whole cities, counties, or metropolitan areas may effectively reduce to impotence any minority which is geographically concentrated.

It would be difficult, at best, to develop a general constitutional rule to govern alike all cases of districting. The Court had not, by the end of its 1964-65 term, sustained any challenge of the selective use of multi-member districts, even when racial motives were alleged to have been the basis of the system.[12] Only one approach

[12] In *Fortson* v. *Dorsey*, 379 U.S. 433 (1965). The Court noted that the racial issue was raised in a challenge to Atlanta's districting system, but it was not pressed, so the Court avoided the issue. In *Hainsworth* v. *Martin*, Court of Civil Appeals of Texas, Austin, No. 11262, Jan. 20, 1965; Rehearing denied Feb. 3, 1965, 386 S.W. 2d 202, Negro voters challenged the use of multi-member districts as discriminatory against their race. The appellate court held that these arguments were political in nature and should be directed to the legislature. The court held that neither the Texas constitution nor the Supreme Court's ruling in *Reynolds* required a state to use single-member districts for legislative elections.

seems to recommend itself as a constitutional rule for such situations. Justice Clark, in his opinion in *Baker,* suggested that "crazy quilt" apportionment patterns which seem to follow no policy should clearly be prohibited by the requirements of the Equal Protection Clause that a rational state policy must be demonstrable.[13] The "crazy quilt" formulation would suggest the rule that a state, in developing districts, must treat all voters alike, and apply whatever pattern it chooses uniformly throughout the state. Beyond this point, however, judging the motives and the effects of particular districting schemes becomes more difficult as the subtleties increase. The "crazy quilt" rule would by no means solve all problems, but it would prevent "averaging out" representation for partisan or interest group advantage, and it would prevent the construction of districts of differing populations (but similar averages per representative) with no rationale apparent in the system.[14]

Each of the problems discussed above tempts further exposition of the democratic theory of the Equal Protection Clause. It would be folly to predict the full extent to which the Court might succumb to the temptations. It is safer to suggest that both the conditions of the cases themselves and the general political climate will greatly affect court response to the unanswered questions. In some of these problems, there is too little development of the democratic creed or the theory of representative government itself to give the Court much guidance in adopting new or extended value mandates as constitutional law. Where there is more nearly a consensus, as with racial gerrymanders, further court action would seem quite probable.

The practical problem deriving from judicial pronouncements on representation is the American tendency—of both the supporters and the detractors of the Court—to substitute rules of law for political theory. The Supreme Court decisions do not provide an *answer* to the basic problems of representative government. They provide only a hint and a challenge to find the full answer.

[13] 369 U.S. 182, 254.

[14] Such a plan was proposed at one point by the Maryland Legislative Council. The plan created nineteen districts, containing from two to fourteen senators. Some of the districts contained populations in excess of a congressional district, and one contained more people than two congressional districts.

THE PRACTICAL POLITICS
OF REAPPORTIONMENT

The image of court-stimulated reapportionment may, in the long run as well as the short run, be as significant as the real changes. While artful constitutional dodges were possible, a considerable transformation in political power seemed certain to occur.

Some practical implications of reapportionment were clear by the time the Dirksen Amendment was defeated. The new state politics of political equality would most strongly affect suburban political power. Analysis of population trends suggested that central cities would ultimately lose representatives along with rural areas.[15] Only a few cities in the country could expect to remain more populous than their own suburbs. While some cities gained seats in the first round of reapportionment following *Baker* and *Reynolds,* almost all cities could expect to lose some seats after 1970.[16]

A second probable consequence of reapportionment was the demise in most states of either urban or rural blocs of legislators of sufficient size to control legislation without assistance from other groupings of lawmakers. By 1965, no city in the country contained a majority of its state's population.[17] In only a few states was there still a rural "majority." In some states, to be sure, a majority of people lived in cities, or in cities and suburbs combined, but such a statistical classification was far removed from any evidence that this would result in an urban or metropolitan bloc. There was much evidence to the contrary.[18] Cincinnati and Cleveland, for example, tended to send representatives of different parties to the Ohio legislature, and New York City and other cities in New York State were occasionally divided by factional lines. Partisan divisions, local patriotism, factionalism, ethnic patterns, and economic differences within single urban areas, between core and suburbs in a single metropolis, and among both separate cities and separate

[15] William J. D. Boyd, "Suburbia Takes Over," *National Civic Review* (June 1965), p. 294.
[16] *Ibid.,* p. 298.
[17] *Ibid.,* p. 294.
[18] Malcolm Jewell, *The State Legislature, Politics and Practice* (New York: Random House, 1962), pp. 60-62.

metropolises suggested that the new politics of reapportionment would be highly pluralistic in character. With no segment of the population clearly dominant in the legislature, reapportionment seemed likely to produce a new pluralism in both legislative and electoral politics.

As the discussion of urban-rural cleavage has already pointed out, there are many diverse interests within both rural and urban areas. It is inaccurate to suppose that suburban voters constitute a homogeneous mass of humanity. Recent studies have shown the diversity of the suburban population to be rather extensive,[19] and suburban diversity is increasing. While agricultural interests were certain to lose representatives directly elected from agricultural constituencies, no such prediction could be made with confidence concerning business-oriented or labor-oriented representatives. While labor expected gains from reapportionment and business generally expected losses in political strength, the character of the gains and losses would not seem to come from "labor" or "business" constituencies. Rather they would appear to result from the pro-education and pro-government action politics of suburban communities. Thus, while farm orientation among legislators would be reduced, some observers expected more support in the new legislatures for "conservation" legislation.[20]

The effect of reapportionment on the group structure of state politics and on party politics depended largely upon the characteristics of the specific reapportionment and redistricting plans employed. The plans employed depended very largely in turn upon the composition of the legislature which produced them. The party most likely to benefit from reapportionment was, therefore, the party in power, if it could get its plans approved by the courts. The New York legislature, under Republican leadership, enacted a plan to provide maximum assistance to its candidates. In Ohio, a plan was devised to improve Republican chances. A federal court approved the New York plan as constitutional, but voters turned down the Ohio referendum after a spirited campaign against it led by the state AFL-CIO.

Whatever the specific partisan result or group benefits, the power

[19] Advisory Commission on Intergovernmental Relations, *Metropolitan Social and Economic Disparities: Implications for Intergovernmental Relations in Cities and Suburbs* (Washington: U.S. Advisory Commission on Intergovernmental Relations, 1965).
[20] 111 *Congressional Record* A2952.

systems of the states were to be altered by reapportionment. The new legislatures would contain not only many members from the new constituencies replacing the old, but many a legislature would find that a majority of its members had never served there before. Combined with the number of new constituencies and the extensive gains of the suburbs over both cities and rural areas, the new legislatures would represent a substantial break with the past. They would be more unstructured, both in their internal relationships and in their relation to the old power systems of the parties and pressure groups. At least for the short run and probably for a fairly extended period, state legislative politics could be expected to exhibit more fluidity than in the past. Given suburban growth trends and the instability of suburban political systems in many areas, a fairly large group of "independent," i.e., "uncontrolled," representatives should find legislative seats.

Finally, reapportionment was sure to affect local governmental systems through extension of the basic rules of *Baker* and *Reynolds* to city councils and county governing bodies. Once again the twin beneficiaries would be suburbs and core city areas with dense population.

REPRESENTATION
IN METROPOLITAN AMERICA

It now is given that personal political equality is the only permissible basis for apportionment of legislative representatives. Majority rule, based on equal representation of equal voters, follows as an assumption of the new system. Given these assumptions, how shall the political system be structured to permit it to meet the problems of modern life through democratic processes and in the context of democratic values? In organizing the political system, the process of representation, as distinguished from the mere basis for it, plays a central role. The problem is to match the functions performed by a representative system with both political values and the conditions and needs of the polity.

Reapportionment merely reflected the fundamental transformation of American society into a highly urbanized, science-oriented, and technologically precocious civilization. With this transformation much disappeared which had provided the basis for traditional ideas of representation.

With the use of the metropolis as the dominant pattern of economic and social relationships, and with the technological revolutions in transportation and communications, the old community patterns have eroded. The metropolis, in many respects, is an antithesis of the "community." Its basic pattern of politics is conflict rather than consensus or common interest. Its economies are specialized and competitive, its society is by comparison with the old villages and towns, unstable. Mobility within the metropolis and among separate metropolitan areas is common. Social mobility is also increasing. Among the residents of any given neighborhood, there is rather extensive mobility of the working force commuting to work. Social relationships, especially among the middle and upper classes, are restricted neither to neighborhood nor even the metropolis itself.

In this new environment, some of the traditional worries of theorists of representative government are sterile. The new politics of technological complexity and urban pluralism is not well defined by the majority-minority dichotomy. There is, for all practical purpose, no MAJORITY; there are only coalitions of minorities. While a party might statistically dominate an urban area, there often is a considerable difference between an electoral majority and a stable governing majority.

With the weakening of the sense of community in the metropolis, the old familiar concepts of constituency also tend to deteriorate. Jurisdictional boundaries are no clue to communities in the metropolis. Legislative constituencies built on residential neighborhoods or political subdivisions in the metropolis are quite likely to fail to reflect either a community of interest or salient relationships or interests of metropolitan life. Such districts, so congenial to tradition and so convenient to established power systems, tend to accentuate class, ethnic, and interjurisdictional conflict, rather than make the legislature a place for the management and resolution of conflict.

But this is one purpose which a representative system ought to attempt. It is not necessary to have a community of interest in order to manage the conflicts of a plural society. It is, however, necessary to organize political power, largely through the official system of representation in such a way that a vested interest is created in resolving conflict rather than in maintaining it.

The organization of consent and the principle of accountability coincide to suggest that the character of the constituency greatly conditions the kind of consent the electorate will grant, and the range of action which the representative can afford to undertake. The mandate of a representative is to be found in the next election, not in the past one. Thus, a tendency for accommodation can be built into a constituency. A representative of a purely suburban district or of a crowded ghetto is more likely to campaign as a parochial spokesman and to serve as a delegate of his constituency than to perform as a broker among interests.

The institution of bicameralism offers some assistance in meeting the problems of constituency construction. While one house may indeed be built from constituencies with a parochial cast, the other can be fashioned from districts which reflect cross-currents of opinion and are heterogeneous in composition. The second house offers the opportunity to cut across jurisdictional boundaries and "neighborhoods" to require representatives to have built into their political strategies different views of the metropolis or the state. And consideration might be given to districts in one house, at least, which are not compact, in the traditional sense, but which radiate from the center of the metropolis or which are narrow columns or sectors of the metropolis encompassing elements from the business and residential core to the fringe areas. Under satisfactory administrative safeguards to prevent partisan or racial gerrymandering, such districts conceivably would produce representatives more sensitive to the realities of metropolitan life than more traditional approaches.

The representative system functions as the basis for the aggregation of interests and management of conflict, but it also functions as one means of socializing the electorate, of integrating people into the political system. These different objectives can be reconciled, although they are not necessarily complementary. A system which is designed for the optimum management of conflict may offer only minimal political socialization.

In the pre-metropolitan state, the single-member and jurisdiction-wide districts were useful in developing a sense of participation and membership in the political community. Before the revolutions in transportation, communications, and environmental sanitation made the modern metropolis possible, relationships tended to be more localized. Voters could meet candidates. Politics was an entertainment. The ward, the district, the town, or the county might actually have resembled a miniature republic. Personal participation in government through direct representation was more nearly possible than it is now. Mobility has created neighborhoods of strangers and jurisdictions without traditions. Mass communications, which can place an assassination in every living room, has become so costly a resource that local and state politics are virtually blacked out in comparison with national and international affairs. And the gossip structure of the commuting community, served by national chain stores and housed in jurisdictional enclaves separated from both employment and evening social contacts, has little to offer that is relevant to the political system in which representatives are chosen.

In this context, alienation from the political process, nonparticipation in the official system of politics, or support for mass movements as an anti-politics reaction appears to be increasing in metropolitan areas. Somehow the representative system must be made relevant to the conditions of the metropolis that call for attention and still accommodate the demands of groups for recognition and meaningful participation in their government. The "representativeness" problem reappears in modern dress.

The objective of constructing a district may be to give its representative an inter-group perspective; to broaden his outlook. Another is to assimilate the groups into the political system, giving them a broader perspective and an education in democratic politics also. But what are the chances of extensive and "responsible" political participation by Negroes in a district where no Negro has a chance to be elected? Such voters are quite likely to feel unrepresented, just as some rural voters accustomed to their "own" representative in the days before *Reynolds* will feel unrepresented under the new apportionments. This attitude is most likely to occur in multi-class and multi-racial districts from which no representative will really be "typical."Again bicameralism, with its larger capacity to incorporate alternate approaches to representation, may provide a workable framework for reconciling the need for representativeness and political socialization with the need for conflict reconciliation.

Another aspect of the problem of representativeness is also a problem in political communications: accessibility of the representative to his constituents. The Dirksen Amendment's backers made this one of their major issues, envisioning great physical distances separating the representative and the voters in the sparsely populated districts. The urban counterpart of the problem is social distance, the crush of business and the cost of communications as well as the competition for electoral attention. The state legislative candidate can rarely afford to use metropolitan television or newspaper advertising. He must depend more largely on direct mailings, organization support, or personal contact. If he has a populous citywide or county-wide constituency, even if shared with other legislators, he cannot become known to most of his constituency. In a city of a half-million people, it is extremely unlikely that a legislator can personally contact or confront more than fifteen per cent of his electorate.

The result of such a districting situation is not only the production of voter alienation due to the inaccessibility of the politicians, but the frequent construction of tickets of legislative candidates loaded with plodding party regulars who can depend for their election on a dependable primary vote, which rarely needs to exceed twenty per cent of all voters registered. The dominant faction of the dominant party tends to win all seats. The election system filters out the conflicts needed to confront the state government with the basic problems of the metropolis. In the bargain, the quality of the legislators is also depressed. One of the cautions in constituency construction, then, is to create no more outsized constituencies than there are likely to be outsized legislators to represent them. The objective of attaining an at-large view of problems can be readily frustrated by the election of members whose crucial pluralities depend upon only a narrow segment of the electorate.[21]

The test of systems of representation will be both in what they produce and how they produce it. The predictable growth of population and the innovations of technology will create functional pressures which government must meet. And it is useful to keep in mind that it is not necessary to have a democracy to make trains run on time or to provide an efficient police force.

Representation, therefore, must be structured to make the system respond to the salient relationships and problems of modern life. A way must be found to permit the people affected by government's acts to hold the government accountable for what it does, and to associate meaningfully with others in conditioning and controlling what government does. Grave functional pressures can be easily foreseen. The availability, accessibility, variety, and cost of housing will be a major problem for both state and federal govern-

[21] For a discussion of the impact of nominating pluralities on the character of legislators and parties, see V. O. Key, Jr., *American State Parties: An Introduction* (New York: Knopf, 1956), pp. 169-96.

ments, as will the problem of racial segregation in housing and other economic activity.

Racial assimilation can be greatly assisted through the structuring of the representative system. While racial frustrations can be allayed by the integration of politics, political integration can also lay foundations for meeting the legal, psychological, and social obstacles to racial equality.

Transportation, as a shaper of cities and regions, is a function upon which much controversy will center. Representative systems which allow expression of suburban interests in commutation and core city interests in the housing, market, and social impact of metropolitan transportation systems are more likely to find an acceptable resolution for transportation problems than systems which box the conflicting interests into segregated power cells.

And in other fields such as personal security and education the quality, type, and extent of programs will reflect the power transmitted through the representative process. The challenge of reapportionment will hardly be met by making only the *pro forma* adjustments necessary to reconcile the old systems of representation with the bare requirements of the Supreme Court's pronouncements.

The future of representative government begins with the constitutional mandate for political equality. The Supreme Court's action was a necessary prelude to rethinking the problem of representative government. It does not assure, however, that the old sterile patterns will be broken. Most of the problems discussed here do not seem susceptible to the development of an official philosophy through the same processes of constitutional politics which produced *Reynolds* and preserved its ruling. The Supreme Court decision institutionalized a value upon which there was extensive agreement. On these other matters, there is no consensus, not even wide agreement. Room for experimentation is needed.

There has been little updating of the political theory of representative government and inertia has ruled both thought and practice. Much advocacy of proportional representation and syndicalism has not met the kind of needs discussed here. The legislature needs to be more than a mere assembly of the ambassadors of interest groups. But now that the inertia has been broken, it is time to re-examine the role representative government should play in the American states. That opportunity presents itself, in all probability, in the series of constitutional conventions which seem likely to follow reapportionment.

The politicians of constitutional democracy devised the strategy which ultimately destroyed the Old Order. Have they the vision, the wit, the courage to fashion the New?

GENERAL BIBLIOGRAPHY

The literature on reapportionment and redistricting, like the growth of a bacterial mold culture, has increased so rapidly that it seems in danger of being consumed by its own waste products. The purpose of this brief bibliography is to indicate a basic, yet comprehensive reading list for anyone who wishes to pursue the subject further and to explore viewpoints other than those expressed in this book.

Alfred De Grazia's *Public and Republic* (New York: Alfred A. Knopf, Inc., 1951), is the best general study of representation in the United States. *Apportionment and Representative Government* by the same author (New York: Frederick A. Praeger, 1963), is primarily a brief against court involvement in the reapportionment controversy and presents a lucid argument for a departure from traditional approaches to legislative representation.

Among the best studies of the apportionment problem as such are Gordon E. Baker's *Rural* v. *Urban Political Power* (Garden City, New York: Doubleday & Company, Inc., 1955) and his *State Constitutions: Reapportionment* (New York: National Municipal League, 1960). To Baker's studies two important additions are essential for the serious student of the problem. Paul T. David's and Ralph Eisenberg's *Devaluation of the Urban and Suburban Vote*, 2 vols. (Charlottesville: Bureau of Administration, University of Virginia, 1961-62) provides a much needed comparative analysis of the reapportionment problem. This study does much to clarify thinking about the dimensions of the problem and suggests means of measuring malapportionment. Shortly after *Baker* v. *Carr*, the U.S. Advisory Commission on Intergovernmental Relations published *Apportionment of State Legislatures* (Washington: ACIR Report A-5, 1962). The general reader might also be interested in *The State Legislature: Politics and Practice* by Malcolm E. Jewell (New York: Random House, 1962).

A second category of literature, and one likely to expand almost endlessly, is found in the case studies of state apportionment controversies. Most of those now in print deal with the problem as it existed before, or at the time of, the reapportionment cases. *The Politics of Reapportionment,* edited by Malcolm E. Jewell (New York: Atherton Press, 1962) con-

136

tains cases on apportionment and districting problems from a variety of states. To this basic and uneven series of case studies a few others should be added. The most thorough analysis is that by William C. Harvard and Loren P. Beth, *The Politics of Mis-representation: Rural-Urban Conflict in the Florida Legislature* (Baton Rouge: Louisiana State University Press, 1962). An excellent treatment of a reapportionment problem is contained in Samuel K. Gove and Gilbert Y. Steiner, *The Legislature Redistricts Illinois* (Urbana: Institute of Government and Public Affairs, University of Illinois, 1956). Two reapportionment case studies have been published by the Eagleton Institute for Practical Politics: Gordon E. Baker, *The Politics of Reapportionment in Washington* (New York: Holt, Rinehart and Winston, Inc., 1960, republished by McGraw-Hill), and Royce Hanson, *Fair Representation Comes to Maryland* (New York: McGraw-Hill Book Company, Inc., 1964).

Almost no self-respecting law review has neglected the reapportionment problem. A must for any student of the subject, however, is Anthony Lewis's challenging "Legislative Apportionment and the Federal Courts," 71 *Harvard Law Review* 1057 (April 1958). After *Baker* almost everyone with a law degree, and many without, seemed to write articles. The best post mortem on *Baker* was conducted by Robert G. Dixon, Jr., "Legislative Apportionment and the Federal Constitution," 27 *Law and Contemporary Problems* 329 (Summer 1962). For views favorable to the reapportionment cases, see C. Herman Pritchett, "Equal Protection and the Urban Majority," *The American Political Science Review*, LVIII (December 1964) 869; Robert B. McKay, "Political Thickets and Crazy Quilts: Reapportionment and Equal Protection," 61 *Michigan Law Review* 645 (February 1963); and Royce Hanson, "Courts in the Thicket: The Problem of Judicial Standards in Apportionment Cases," 12 *American University Law Review* 51 (January 1963).

For more pessimistic views of court involvement in reapportionment and redistricting controversies, see: Robert G. McCloskey, "Forward: The Reapportionment Case," 76 *Harvard Law Review* 54 (November 1962); Alexander M. Bickel, "The Durability of Colegrove v. Green," 72 *Yale Law Journal* 39 (November 1962); and Robert G. Dixon, Jr., "Reapportionment Perspectives: What Is Fair Representation?" 51 *American Bar Association Journal* 319 (April 1965).

After all this, the reader still hungry for materials can always consult the National Municipal League's ever growing compendium of all the reapportionment cases: *Court Decisions on Legislative Apportionment* (New York: National Municipal League, 1962-   ). The only "compact" source yet available for study of the Dirksen Amendment are the hearings: U.S. Congress, Senate Subcommittee on Constitutional Amendments, *Reapportionment of State Legislatures*, 89th Congress, 1st Session (Washington: U.S. Government Printing Office, 1965).